iPhone 11

The Complete User Manual For Dummies, Beginners, and Seniors

(The User Manual like No Other (4th Edition))

Phila Perry

Published By:

ENGOLEE PUBLISHING HOUSE

Website: www.engolee.com/bookdeals

Email: info@engolee.com

Table of Contents

FREE BONUS

Are you passionate about reading and adding new value to yourself? Would you love to get various **FREE & DISCOUNTED** books delivered to your inbox courtesy of **Engolee Publishing House**?

GET ACCESS NOW!

or

Visit http://www.engolee.com/bookdeals

OTHER BOOKS BY THE SAME AUTHOR

Before we proceed, I'd like to say thank you for downloading and buying this book. I believe the information would impact your life significantly. Please find below the other books I have written, which are impactful.

1. iPad: The User Manual like No Other

2. iPhone: The User Manual like No Other

3. iPhone 6s: A Guide To iPhone 6S for All Ages: The User Manual like No Other

4. iPhone 6s Plus: The Ultimate Guide to Revolutionizing Your iPhone Mobile: The User Manual like No Other

5. Apple Watch Series: The Ultimate Guide For All Apple Watch Band Series Users: The User manual Like No Other

6. iPad Pro: The Beginners, Kids and Expert Guide to iPad Pro 12.9 and Other Versions: The User

Manual like No Other

Visit to follow the Author's page and See all other books by the Author:

https://amazon.com/author/philaperry

Introduction

Are you new to iPhone 11, iPhone 11 Pro, and iPhone 11 Pro max?

This book shows you new and exciting tips and in-depth tutorials you need to know about the new iPhone 11 features and the iOS 13 user interface.

This guide is packed with top tips and in-depth tutorials. You'll uncover the exclusive features of this new iPhone, learn how to take incredible photos, learn how to start dark mode settings and customize your phone, discover how to use iOS 13, how to create and use iPhone 11 shortcuts and gestures, and its built-in apps, plus much more.

In this book you'll discover:

• How to set up your brand new iPhone

• How to Use Look Around feature in Apple Maps

• How to Customize Your Memoji and Animoji

• How to Use the New Gestures for Copy, Cut, Paste, Redo and Undo

• How to Use Cycle Tracking in Health

• iPhone 11 tips and tricks tutorials

- Software & hardware features of iPhone 11

- In-depth coverage of iOS 13

- Top iPhone gestures and shortcuts

- New Homepod features

- Difference between iPhone 11 & iPhone X

- Detailed app tutorials

- The secrets of mastering mobile photography

- How to edit photos

- Essential Settings and configurations

- Troubleshooting tips

- How to Enable Dark Mode.

…and many more!

This book is the best user manual you need to guide you on how to use and optimally maximize your iPhone.

This book has ***comprehensive tips & in-depth tutorials*** for beginners, dummies, seniors, kids, teens, and adults. By the time you've finished reading this book, you'll be a pro in nearly everything related to iPhone and iOS.

Chapter 1

The iPhone 11 and iPhone 11 Pro

It took me a defeat to understand the new iPhone 11, in fact, Apple's successor to the iPhone XR rather than the offspring of the high-end iPhone XS; this subtle shift in the merchandise line, which walks from the iPhone "X" model and also repositions the baseline iPhone as a slightly less able device that you can purchase for a considerable number of dollars significantly lesser than Apple's most effective smartphone, maybe Apple's smartest little bit of rebranding.

iPhone 11

iPhone 11 Pro

iPhone 11 Pro Max

iPhone 11	iPhone 11 Pro	iPhone 11 Pro Max
6.1-inch LCD	5.8-inch OLED	6.5-inch OLED
1792 x 828 at 326 ppi	2436 x 1125 at 458 ppi	2688 x 1242 at 458 ppi
No 3D Touch	No 3D Touch	No 3D Touch
Face ID	Face ID	Face ID
A13 Chip	A13 Chip	A13 Chip
4GB RAM	6GB RAM	6GB RAM
12MP front camera	12MP front camera	12MP front camera
Dual 12MP rear cameras	Triple 12MP rear cameras	Triple 12MP rear cameras
Bilateral wireless charging	Bilateral wireless charging	Bilateral wireless charging
WiFi 6	WiFi 6	WiFi 6
No Apple Pencil support	Apple Pencil support	Apple Pencil support
Glass design	Frost glass design	Frost glass design
3,110 mAh battery	3,190+ mAh battery	3,500+ mAh battery
64GB/256GB/512GB	128GB/256GB/512GB	128GB/256GB/512GB
Starting at $749	**Starting at $999**	**Starting at $1099**

Apple Design Heading a Different Way

Labels aren't as important as the design and features, and no matter which new iPhone 11 you choose-if you select one-Apple, they will provide good video cameras, more electric battery life, better level of resistance to the elements and, of course, they'll all dispatch with iOS 13, that includes a lot of useful mobile operating-system updates.

I noticed lots of people who comment on Twitter weren't kind to the new design on iPhone 11, as they perceived it as a clunky design choice, but they're responding to photos of the device.

The iPhone 11 Camera

I handled all three cell phones, and the camera arrays are distinctive, they don't stick out just as much as you'd think; this is due to the somewhat surprising process Apple uses to produce the iPhone 11 and iPhone 11 Pro back, it is just one piece of cup (a brushed back on the iPhone 11 Pro and shiny on the iPhone 11) that Apple milled down while departing the camera array elevated.

It's the type of design many people will readily make to access Apple's new 120-level field of view ultra-wide 12 MP camera, which is on both models. All iPhone 11 models likewise have a typical wide-angle 12 MP camera. The iPhone 11 Pro provides the 2X optical focus camera.

All of those other design, incidentally, is unchanged. All of the mobile phones still have the notch for the True depth Component, which now includes a 12 MP selfie camera with the capacity of slow-motion video for "selfies.

Display Screen Technology

I doubt if anyone could tell the difference between iPhone 11 and iPhone XR, XS, and XS Max, which includes the same screen technology and quality as the iPhone XR. Apple upgrades the body of all the cell phones, as *iPhone 11 can handle thirty minutes under 2 meters of water, and iPhone 11 Pro can handle thirty minutes under 4 meters of water*; this appears to be that they're ready for a swim.

Just like the iPhone XR, the iPhone 11 gets the majority

of the cool colours; however, the metal iPhone 11 Pro is no slouch: It gets a new Midnight-Green option (exquisite). Each one of these devices seems excellent and stable in hands. I especially liked the feel of the iPhone 11 Pro's brushed cup back.

Apple, naturally, pushed the visual envelope on the $999 iPhone 11 Pro, which includes what's called a brilliant Retina *XDR screen* (it's **OLED**), which is a name that needs to be familiar to the people who followed the Mac PC Pro information from earlier this year 2019. I don't know if the eye can visually process *458 PPI*, but I'll say that the images and video (*up to 4K 60 FPS*) on the iPhone 11 Pro were stunning. Also, the audio, which now helps Dolby Atmos, was almost noisy enough to conquer the very occupied demo room.

Improving the Camera App

Consumers might be most thinking about the amount of change apple has infiltrated in camera and video applications to aid all the new *iPhone 11, iPhone 11 pro* and *iPhone 11 Pro* max photographic features. Rather than hard switches between lens, Apple redesigned the native apps to aid smooth transitions with swipes and arc scrolls.

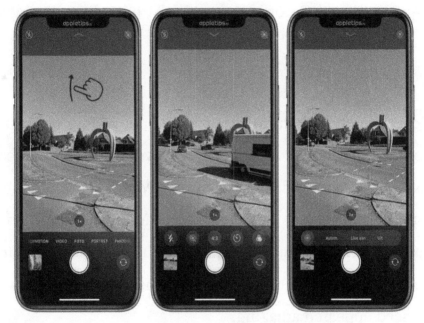

Apple's Phil Schiller before the projected image of a three-camera selection of iPhone 11 Pro

To place a more exceptional point on the Camera Apps requires continuous knowledge on all the lenses, the standard picture window concurrently shows the ultra-wide image in the greyed-out areas on either part of the picture.

You can view instantly how an ultra-wide shot might look; furthermore, the indigenous video app is now able to do some aesthetic video edits, controlling brightness, comparison, and even permitting you to crop your video (sometimes you won't realize how much you skipped it until you begin cropping randomly out of your video backgrounds).

Several picture features represent Apple getting up to its competitors, but at least Apple always manages to place its spin on the updates. Regarding *Night Mode Setting*, Apple has finally made the feature automated, which is smart because most consumers don't want to take into account photo changing configurations. The test images I noticed appeared amazing.

A13 Bionic CPU

Apple's new *A13 Bionic CPU* has *8.5 billion processors*, which it uses to do some pretty impressive image-processing gymnastics; it can help the iPhone 11 execute a trillion procedures on each image, but I have been intrigued with what Apple says is arriving later, which is called *"Deep Fusion,"* this is a leading-edge. *Neural Engine-backed* procedure somehow requires nine photos before you even press the shutter, the engine then creates one properly uncovered and detail-rich picture out of everything. It seems crazy, and I'm just a little unfortunate that we'll have to hold back for Apple to include it to the *iPhone 11 Pro*.

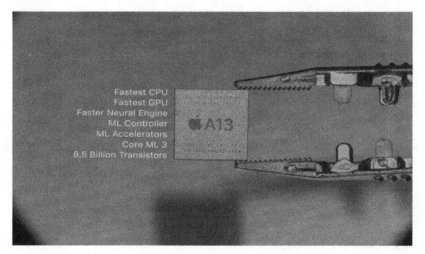

Regardless of the increased power, Apple claims that the iPhone 11 Pro gets 4 hours more battery life than the iPhone XS Max. I usually take these electric battery performance statements with a grain of sodium. However, battery life mainly depends on what you're doing with the phone.

What wasn't told about iPhone 11

Oddly, there is no reference to new wireless charging features. Everyone expected Apple to unveil something such as *Samsung's cellular PowerShare*, which would've to allow iPhone share power, wirelessly charging AirPod 2 devices. Apple also mentioned improved Face Identification Speed multiple times while preventing the apparent fingerprint. It appears that Apple may soon be the only major smartphone producer who's not concealing biometric security.

Finally, there is not a single reference to 5G technology; 5G would strike NEW YORK and other major urban centres throughout the year 2020. Apple made a technique that required the ultra-popular XR and improved it with another camera and the latest CPU while keeping the purchase price at $699, and it forced the envelope on the iPhone 11 Pro Max.

Chapter 2

iPhone 11 Pro Overview

Home devices are so organic. It's a disservice to see them through an individual attribute; for instance, calling the iPhone 11 Pro and iPhone 11 Pro Max "cell phones" or even smartphones is reductive. At best, they're pocketable computer systems with communication, content catch, and posting with efficient features.

Yet, when people navigate the new handsets, which Apple unveiled on Sept 10 in Cupertino, CA, all they can easily see is the three-camera zoom lens construction seated in an elevated cup square on the trunk of every device.

iPhone 11 Pro and iPhone 11 Pro Max

Apart from size, the iPhone 11 Pro (foreground) and the iPhone 11 Pro Max are identical electronically. They are Reduced to a meme, the iPhone 11 Pro and iPhone Pro Max might run into a significant misstep in Apple's decade-plus through smartphone developing design and development jobs, but that might be a misreading of reality.

Studying a large number of friendly media responses to my first photos of the 5.8-inch iPhone 11 Pro and 6.5-inch iPhone 11 Pro Max, I became confident of the fact that the merchandise looked different in pictures than it looks physically. Why I wouldn't call the camera square beautiful; it is durable, telegraphing its photographic motives and features to anyone who cares.

Apart from the radical camera component redesign, Apple didn't stray the iPhone body design, vocabulary introduced with the iPhone 6, which has continued to last years before iPhone XS. Apple's iPhone 11 Pro ($999, 64

GB) and 11 Pro Max ($1,099 64 GB) feature lots of the same recognizable curves on the iPhone XS.

Bottom level end of the iPhone 11 Pro and iPhone 11 Pro Max

Apple hasn't transformed the port, mic, or speaker settings on the iPhone 11 Pro and iPhone 11 Pro Max. Departing aside for an instant, the display technology changes; Apple didn't even change the display screen design, all of the new iPhones still feature the TrueDepth notch within a normally unblemished, almost edge-to-edge display.

iPhone 11 Pro in Hand

Aside from an original 12 MP camera, the real Depth notch is unchanged. However, what will be more noticeable within the last couple of years is that these new devices have added on just a little weight. Apple does not focus on the weight and width of their iPhones, in virtually any meaningful way. That's because being the thinnest didn't gain them anything (keep in mind when individuals were purposely twisting their 6.9 mm-thin iPhones?).

At 144 mm high by 71.4 mm wide by 8.1 mm deep, the 5.8-inch iPhone 11 Pro is slightly bigger than the iPhone XS and noticeably thicker than last year's 7.7 mm smartphone. The story plot is the same on the bigger 6.5-inch iPhone 11 Pro Max. It's 158 mm by 77.8 mm by 8.1 mm thick. With 226 grams, it's 18 grams heavier than the iPhone XS Max.

iPhone 11 Pro Stacked atop iPhone 11 Pro Max

The iPhone 11 Pro and iPhone 11 Pro Max are somewhat thicker, larger, and more substantial than the XS series. Dimension-wise, the new iPhone 11 Pro and iPhone 11 Pro max don't feel much different; however, the added width and weight are unmistakable and don't even try to evaluate it to a bigger-screen 6.8-inch Samsung Galaxy Notice10+. Samsung's handset is both slimmer (7.9 mm) and significantly lighter (196 grams) than small-screened iPhone 11 Pro Max, while still including an S-Pen stylus.

iPhone 11 Pro held aloft in hand

The iPhone 11 Pro trunk is a brushed cup, polished on the rectangular camera. Notice, also, that the term "iPhone" has vanished once more from the back. I'm not implying that either iPhone 11 Pro is uncomfortable to carry; I'm especially keen on the brushed cup back on the iPhone 11 Pro max, which is on the rigid-still, somewhat torque-able-stainless steel framework - it feels good, appears razor-sharp, and hides your fingerprints completely. Apple's 6.1-inch iPhone 11, incidentally, features clean glass that still does a much better job of hiding fingerprints than the Gorilla Glass on the Samsung Galaxy Note 10+. Although the iPhone 11 Pro body isn't wildly the same as the iPhone XS but can sustain longer in water; the iPhone 11 Pro may survive thirty minutes in up to 4 meters of water.

I didn't have a deep pool open to me, but to ensure that the iPhone 11 Pro could deal with at least a dunk in the bathroom, I filled a cooler with about 2 ft of water and dropped both iPhone 11 Pro models; they easily survived ten minutes in the water.

iPhone 11 Pro submerged in water

Both the iPhone 11 and iPhone 11 Pro Potentially handled my water test like champs. Rather than wasting time wanting to persuade you that the iPhone 11 Pro camera module is much less unsightly as you believe that it is, I'd instead concentrate on the engineering feat it took to produce that raised package. The back is, in fact, one continuous bit of cup milled around the elevated square; it's a beautiful materials design down the cup circles encircling the three large lenses, and more significant True Firmness LED adobe flash and microphone openings. The cup will not cover the lens; instead, Apple is once more using Sapphire Crystal on all three, providing them with almost as much sapphire as you will probably find on the $749 Apple Watch face.

I love Apple's **Face ID** technology and its secure smart way to unlock, log in to online services, and make obligations. But Apple's devotion to Face technology means that the TrueDepth module notch survives multiple iPhone decades even as competition is pressing everything off leading of their smartphones and only edge-to-edge and infinity displays. Others are drilling microscopic holes in their display screen to support selfie digital cameras (**OnePlus** put its selfie camera in a dangerous, mechanized pop-up camera component, leaving its display screen unblemished). Apple states that Face Identification recognition is even faster than before. It is rapid and constant, but, at least in my assessments, not noticeably faster. I did so detect somewhat better off-angle face recognition.

I've now examined multiple Google android smartphones with an under-the-screen fingerprint sensor; while none of these is perfect, each of them works very well enough. To become reasonable to Apple, though, none of the competition ever built what I consider "near fool-proof face recognition technology."

iPhone 11 Pro and iPhone 11 Pro Max on Display Screen.

Apple's smartphones will have one of the very most noticeable dark bezels around their displays, at least in comparison with the *Samsung Galaxy Note 10+* and the *OnePlus 7 Pro*, both of which use curved displays to extend the edges of their screen visually.

There's also no iPhone 11 Pro or iPhone 11 Pro Max 5G option. Here, I believe Apple's made the right choice; 5G is a complicated and mostly non-existent clutter in the U.S. and probably won't suffice for another 12 months. At that time, Apple will have its 5G iPhone 12.

Screen Time

If we pass the figures, Apple's OLED Super Retina XDR screen is, at 458 ppi 2436x1125 pixels, not the sharpest smartphone screen on the marketplace. The 498 ppi Galaxy Notice 10+ keeps that honour; they are doing a match on the two 2,000,000:1 comparison ratio.

Apple's premiere smartphone now includes a Super Retina XDR screen. However, this a beautiful display screen, especially on the bigger device (2688x1242 pixels). The rise to 800 nits lighting (up to at least one 1,200 nits maximum) is incidentally noticeable entirely at daylight, at least when compared with the iPhone XS.

Perhaps the easiest way to see the display's stunning visual quality is by viewing 4K 60 FPS video. I shot some of the iPhone 11 Pro and was startled by the hyper-realism. Even on the tiny smartphone display. I've hardly ever really griped about the notch.

However, when a display is this good, it's a pity to devote the area to other things. The iPhone 11 Pro also marks the finish of 3D Touch; this under-the-screen technology held tabs on how hard you pressed on the display screen and would start additional, quick-access features on, say, the Camera application of the phone recognized more pressure as you kept your finger on the icon for a couple of seconds. The iPhone 11 Pro (as well as iPhone 11 Pro Max and standard 11 models) now use Haptic Touch exclusively, and you now have to press just a little much longer to access a few of these features and, in some instances, in specific places.

My thumb typing is abysmal, and I've relied on 3D Touch to press the keyboard display and gain fast access to the keyboard mouse, which let me split my finger around on the keyboard (as though it was on the trackpad), putting the cursor wherever I have to write. With Haptic Touch, I must press precisely on the area bar to trigger the digital trackpad (It's an annoyance that I'm already modifying to).

Camera Love for iPhone 11 Pro and iPhone 11 Pro Max

Whatever it is you like about the iPhone 11 Pro and 11 Pro Max camera design would fade when you begin using them. Nowadays, there are three 12 MP cameras at the back of the iPhone 11 Pro (apart from the size, all specs on the iPhone 11 Pro Max are similar, so my comments using one address both products).

Nowadays, there are four 12 MP digital cameras on these devices if you count number the main one in the TrueDepth component in front. There's the:

- *12 MP Wide (f/1.8 aperture)*

- *12 MP Ultra Wide (f/2.4 aperture with a 120-level field of view)*

- *12 MP Telephoto (f/2.0 aperture)*

Instantly, many of these lenses are bigger than those on the iPhone XS and XS Max; the brand new ultra-wide is a six-element lens, as the wide and telephoto are both five-element lenses.

A wide-angle view of that time Square

Most of them make excellent, colour-accurate, and detailed images. Apple is past due to the overall game with an ultra-wide zoom lens, but Apple brought its A-Game. Along with standard photos, you may use the ultra-wide zoom lens in the video, time-lapse (making them a lot more dramatic), and breathtaking, which creates an almost 360-level photo effect.

Capturing panorama photos in super-wide creates a near 360-level impact. Considering just how many selfies most of us take, getting the front-facing camera good (it's now 12 MP with an f/2.2 aperture) was a good move ahead of Apple's part.

I was impressed with the image quality, especially *family portrait mode*. With all the front-facing camera, you can also achieve a somewhat more wide position impact by tapping a set of arrow symbols on the display screen; this isn't a focus out or traditional wide position; instead, the camera is switching from hook crop of the entire 12 MP framework to a full-frame image, which enables you to pull more folks into the group selfie.

The very best part is that if you turn the camera to scenery orientation, the selfie camera automatically adjusts to full-frame. *The camera is also now with the capacity of shooting 4K 60 fps video, that I think is a boon for YouTubers who prefer to have the live-screen feedback while they shoot but hate sacrificing video quality (Now they can have both).*

It certainly nice when you're able to have a pro-level picture with one hand.

Just like the iPhone XR before it, the iPhone 11 Pro is now able to use the wide zoom lens to get more dramatic Family Portrait Mode images. The iPhone XS would combine both wide and telephoto, which design you always need to step back from your subject matter.

Camera Application Updated

To support each one of these new lens and photography options, Apple significantly updates its camera app.

iPhone 11 Pro Camera App

Rather than 1X and 2X and the primary zoom options, nowadays, there are three with ultra-wide, represented as a "0.5x" or fifty percent focus. It's choice I find just a little complication since Samsung describes its three capturing settings with a stand of trees and shrubs: one tree represents 2X, two represents no move, and a relatively distant band of three trees and shrubs represents ultra-wide (I honestly can't decide which is clearer).

Even if you're not in the iPhone 11 Pro's new ultra-wide camera mode, the new camera application will always demonstrate the amount of visual information you're abandoning: the dark borders of the camera application turn translucent, and that means you can see the actual ultra-wide zoom lens, which would be added if you were utilizing it.

Apple, also has introduced a Camera App drawer that you gain access to by swiping up close to the bottom level of the display. Under it, is aspect percentage *(4:3 or 16:9), Live photos, display screen, filters, HDR*, as well as your timer (I had been a little annoyed that Apple hid it this way). I love the new QuickTake video feature, which enables you to switch from picture set to video by just keeping down the shutter button. After that, you can slip it to lock it on while keeping the usage of a photo-in-video button on the right.

Probably the most exciting camera update, though, is ***Night mode*** (Apple's first feature-level effort with low-light photography). In this field, too, Apple is playing catch-up but with some rather stunning results.

Would you like to dance in the Pale Moonlight?
Night mode is not at all something you decide; instead, the iPhone 11 Pro automatically get on Night setting in low-light situations. It's indicated with a yellowish,

eclipse-like icon in the top left-hand part of the Camera application screen.

Night mode comparison shot of the yellow bike in a shed

I took all three of the photos that was essentially a pitch dark shed; all three were able to catch a great deal of fine detail, but I believe Apple's Night setting gets the best balance of colour and clearness, Among the things I believe many people are surprised to find themselves using night time photo features on other mobile phones like Samsung's Galaxy collection and the Google Pixel; however, the dark requires the smartphone camera shutter to remain open for a couple of seconds and that you should stand still.

Night mode shot of the moon

In Nighttime mode, Apple offers a few of the most explicit help with ways to get the best ultra-low-light shot. I took photos in dark areas, enclosed almost lightless rooms, during the night; evening Setting instructed me to "Keep Still" as it modified the amount of time it would keep open up the shutter (usually, this between three and five seconds; you can view the shutter timer by gradually scrolling down). You can even either manually set the shutter to stay open up for 28 seconds to fully capture light paths or, if you place the smartphone on the tripod, allow the shutter to automatically opens up longer to fully capture.

iPhone 11 Pro Night shot with stars in the sky
Through a side-by-side-by-side test with the Google Pixel 3 and the Samsung Galaxy Notice 10+, Apple's iPhone 11 Pro Max produced the clearest Night mode shot. All three photos were good, but the Note10+ launched a lot of sound to the image and the Pixel 3 sacrificed some details for brightness.

Assessment of backlit selfie from iPhone 11 Pro and Galaxy Note 10+

I don't believe there's any question of 12 MP selfie camera doing a much better job here. The colours on the iPhone 11 Pro shot are accurate and, even in darkness, the facts on my face and throat are there. I did so, incidentally, switch off Samsung's default pores and skin filter to get the most accurate shot.

I'm also impressed with the changes Apple's designed to Smart HDR. Backlight photography is much better than what I possibly could achieve with my DSLR, which is without an adobe flash. In evaluations with Samsung's Galaxy Note 10+, the iPhone 11 Pro was able to accurately catch shadowed details lost or almost glossed over by rivals.

Self Family portrait in High-key Light Mono setting on iPhone 11 Pro

Apple, in addition, has improved the front-facing Portrait Setting photography algorithms. Despite having the new High Key mono setting, Apple was able to find the advantage of my bald mind and produce what appears to be studio-quality photos.

Capacity to Burn

You would believe that, right now, Qualcomm can achieve some parity with Apple, but Apple's bespoke silicon regularly stays a step before virtually all the mobile CPU manufacturers. Backed by, Geekbench, 3.68 GB of RAM, Apple's new A13 Bionic CPUs Geekbench 5 scores are significantly higher than those of the Qualcomm Snapdragon 855 mobile CPU.

Benchmarks

To place these quantities in framework, I played CPU-taxing video games like *Player Unknown's Battlegrounds and Asphalt 9*: Legends, and edited video, including 4K videos, on the iPhone 11 Pro with no issues. Asphalt, specifically, appeared amazing on the Super Retina XDR display screen.

Sound is going Spatial

The iPhone 11 Pro works just fine as a phone. Call quality is clear, and the sound held up perfectly in stiff airflow. Music sounds great on the iPhone 11 Pro's stereo system speakers (the first at the bottom of these devices, the other is within the TrueDepth Component). Yes, it can get noisy, but what's fascinating is the new spatial audio.

iOS 13

The new iPhone 11 Pro (combined with the Pro Max and iPhone 11) comes with iOS 13. Apple's up-to-date mobile operating-system is filled with improvements, large and small. I've been running the beta on an iPhone XS for months and am still stumbling on new features and tiny adjustments.

Naturally, the mixture of iOS 13 and the latest iPhones is

a perfect marriage. There will be the Camera mentioned above application updates, such as new portrait mode tools for adjusting essential light intensity, and they're paired with a completely new Photos app. Photos are currently a far more visually engaging native application that mixes in the image thumbnail sizes and includes video; it will pre-play videos. There's also the new "*For You Personally*" tab that helpfully suggests shareable images. It's also where Apple collects your curated memories. It made a pleasant video out of all my Apple event images.

iPhone Home display in Dark Setting and improved Photos interface.

 The much remaining is the iPhone home display screen in Dark Setting; next to it are two displays from the new Photos "*For You Personally*" tab, which got the long-awaited Dark Setting, and you can now quickly toggle it off by haptic-pressing the screen brightness control at the middle. I've never comprehended the obsession with Dark Mode, which means this is nice-to-have but, for me, at least, not-super-necessary upgrade.

Video Editing display on iPhone in iOS 13

I'm more impressed by the new local and non-destructive video editing tools, that are accessible through either the Camera application or in Photos. You've been able to cut videos and, with slow motion, change where the gradual effect starts and ends. You will adjust brightness, comparison, saturation, sharpness, sound decrease, and more. The best new indigenous video editing feature is cropping, which includes video styling, distortion, rotation, and flipping. There are a great number of third-party video applications that are going to get Sherlocked.

MAPS UPDATE

Apple also updated the Maps App, full disclosure: I take advantage of Apple maps on my iPhone at all times (the turn-by-turn directions I can get on my linked Apple Watch are priceless). iOS 13 provides real-time transit improvements (not that useful in NEW YORK where subway trains usually arrive every short while) and the powerful new *SHOP AROUND* feature.

Apple Maps SHOP AROUND street view

The look Around is nearly the same as Google's Road view, but with far better imagery. It isn't available almost everywhere, though. I came across good coverage for the *San Francisco Bay Area*, but none for *Manhattan*. Apple programs to move out more coverage by the end of the entire year.

In iOS 13, Siri's male and feminine voices do sound more natural, and I might begin using Siri Shortcuts, given that they're pre-installed in the iOS. I used the Shortcuts application to make a shortcut called "Distance to home," which, when I say, "Hey Siri, Distance to Home," would instantly calculate and show me what lengths it is from my current location to my home.

iOS 13 includes Plenty of Enhancements

There are a large number of other feature enhancements in iOS 13, including CarPlay Dashboard and the new Quick Path keyboard, which enables you to swipe across the virtual keyboard to type. I know many people love this feature on Android phones, but I could not get used to using it and still found typing the old-fashioned way faster and easier.

Apple, in addition, has added lots of new Animoji heroes, including an octopus and a cow. The best, though, will be the new Memoji Stickers, which combine common emoji expressions with your personal Animoji and that you can submit host to emojis via *iMessage, FaceTime*, and other apps. A few of iOS 13's better features, like Apple to Remain, where you may use your Apple ID to sign onto other applications and services, and advanced ARKit 3 tools like body tracking and individuals occlusion mostly await developers to introduce them in their apps. I did, however, see an early example of individuals occlusion in the Friends 25 app. It shows real potential.

Overall, I'd say this one of Apple's better OS updates. It manages to make significant system changes without somehow making the system unrecognizable.

Long Electric Battery Life

Unlike its smartphone competitors, Apple doesn't prefer to list the precise specifications of its iPhone batteries. So we're left with somewhat hazy guarantees like the iPhone 11 Pro *"continues 4 hours much longer than the iPhone XS"*, and the iPhone 11 Pro Maximum *"endures up to 5 hours much longer than the iPhone XS Max extent."* The truth is, I'd become more frustrated if these claims weren't right.

When I set up my new iPhone 11 Pro, I did so utilizing the backup from my previous iPhone; this intended the phone spending hours downloading old photos, videos, configurations, and apps, which wiped out your day One electric battery life. I attempted never to judge the phone too harshly because I've experienced this before with earlier new iPhones. By the next day, my iPhone 11 Pro was fully restored and, I didn't recharge it till the following morning; So, it's given me a day-plus about the same charge.

Indeed, I didn't do anything with the phone while I was sleeping, so we must slice out 9 hours of standby setting. So, let's say I acquired about 20 hours, and that is with turning Car Lock off and establishing screen lighting to near maximum. I did a similar thing, incidentally, with the top iPhone 11 Pro Max. As I write this, the iPhone 11 Pro has about 5% power staying and the iPhone 11 Pro Max has about 10%.

I did so not do anything special for doing that electric battery performance, but I also didn't, for example, play video gaming for 20-plus hours. I did so watch a two-hour movie at one point, but I also browsed the net, checked interpersonal media, took a lot of photos and video, paid attention to music, played games, and used several other apps. As always, your battery performance will change predicated on your own iPhone 11 Pro activities.

18W charger for new iPhone 11 Pro and Pro Max

Using the iPhone 11 Pro, Apple carries a redesigned charger for the very first time since switching to the lighting interface; this is Apple's first 18w fast charger for the iPhone; on one end of the included wire is the standard light charger that plugs into the bottom level of the iPhone, but on the other part is a USB-C plug and slot. Someday, I'm confident that Apple will change the iPhone to all USB-C. In a little more than an hour, the iPhone 11 Pro Max was nearly completely charged.

There's still wireless charging, which works efficiently with any Qi-based charger, but no wireless charge share. I was getting excited about putting my capable-of-charging-wirelessly AirPods 2 on the back of the iPhone 11 Pro, mainly because the phone now seems to have the juice to burn off. Apple has made a few changes to connection technology, including updating the Wi-fi to 802.11ax WiFi 6 and adding an Ultra-wideband (UWB) chip for spatial awareness. Eventually, you'll be able to immediate AirDrops by directing your iPhone at a particular recipient.

It's EXCELLENT

No more the thinnest, lightest, or even prettiest smartphone (it was never the least expensive), Apple appears prepared to rely increasingly more on people's devotion to the system (and its growing selection of services) and their desire to have excellent photography.

The iPhone 11 Pro and much larger iPhone 11 Pro max are undoubtedly excellent smartphones, but they're built with an ageing chassis design that feels as though it's looking for an overhaul. Also, Apple made a blunder not starting the bottom models with 128 GB of storage space. I don't expect one to choose the new iPhone since they want showing off their new camera square; however, they will upgrade for the new, formidable camera features.

Chapter 3

How to Set up Your brand-new iPhone 11

For many individuals, the iPhone 11 Series would radically not be the same as the previous iPhone model. Not surprisingly, the iPhone set up process hasn't transformed much. However, you might end up on the familiar ground; you may still find a lot of little things you honestly must do before you switch ON your new phone for the very first time (or soon after that).

Let's check out how to set up your brand-new iPhone 11 the proper way.

Setup iPhone 11 the Correct Way

With iPhone 11, you'll have the ability to take benefit of Apple's Automatic Setup. If you're on an updated iPhone without Face Identification, you would see that Touch ID is entirely gone. (Which means you'll save one face, rather than several.)

If you're a serial upgrader, and you're from the year-old

iPhone X, less has changed. But you'll still need to update just as usual.

iPhone 11 Set up: The Fundamentals

Re-download only the applications you would need; that one is crucial. Most of us have so many applications on our iPhones that people do not use; this is the big reason we execute a clean set up, in all honesty. Utilize the App Store application and make sure you're authorised into the Apple accounts. (Touch the tiny icon of the Updates - panel to see which accounts you're logged on to.) Only download applications you've found in the past half a year. Or, be daring: download stuff you Utilize regularly. We're prepared to wager it'll be considered a very few.

Set up **DO NOT Disturb** - If you're like ordinary people, you're constantly getting notifications, iMessages, and other types of distractions through to your iPhone. Create **DO NOT Disturb** in the Configurations application (it's in the next section listed below, slightly below *Notifications* and *Control Centre*). You'll want to routine it for occasions when you need never to be bothered.

Toggle Alarm to On and then Messages when you want to keep Notifications away from that person. Try 9 p.m. to 8 a.m. when you can.

Pro suggestion: *Let some things through if there's an Emergency: Enable Allow Phone calls From your Favourites and toggle Repeated Phone calls to On. iOS 13 also enables you to switch on DO NOT Disturb at Bedtime, which mutes all notifications and even hides them from the lock screen, and that means you don't get distracted when you take the phone to check the time.*

Auto Setup for iPhone 11

Secondly; Auto Setup enables you to duplicate your Apple ID and home Wi-Fi configurations from another device, simply by getting them close collectively.

In case your old iPhone (or iPad) has already been operating iOS 12 or iOS 13, to put it simply the devices next to one another. Then follow the prompts to avoid needing to enter your Apple ID and Wi-Fi passwords;

this makes the original iPhone set up much smoother.

Set up a fresh iPhone 11 from Scratch

The guide below assumes you're establishing your brand-new iPhone from scratch. If you don't wish to accomplish that, you'll need to acquire any of the other iPhone manuals for beginners that I have written.

Restoring from a back-up of Your old iPhone

You'll probably be restoring your brand-new iPhone from a back-up of your present iPhone. If that's so, then you merely want to do a couple of things:

- Be sure you come with an up-to-date backup.

- Use Apple's new Auto Setup feature to get you started.

The first thing is as simple as going to the iCloud configurations on your iPhone, and looking at that, they're surely a recent automated back-up. If not, do one by hand. Head to *Configurations > Your Name > iCloud > iCloud Back-up and tap **BACKUP Now***. Wait around until it is done.

Set up Face ID

Face ID is much simpler to use than Touch ID, and it's

also simpler to create. Instead of needing to touch your iPhone with your fingerprints, one at a time, you simply check out the camera, and that's almost it. To create Face ID on your iPhone, do the next when prompted through the preliminary iPhone setup. (If you'd like to begin over with a phone you set up previously, check out *Settings > Face ID & Passcode, and type in your password, to begin.*)

Establishing Face ID is similar to the compass calibration your iPhone enables you to do from time to time when you use the Maps app. Only rather than rolling the iPhone around, you turn your head. You'll need to do two scans, and then the iPhone 11 would have your 3D head stored in its Secure Enclave, inaccessible to anything, even to iOS itself (despite some clickbait "news" stories).

Now, still, in Settings/*Configurations > Face ID & Passcode*, you can pick which features to use with Face ID, as everyone else did with *Touch ID*.

If you regularly sport another appearance - you're a

clown, a doctor, an impersonator, or something similar - then additionally, you should create another impression. Just tap the button in the facial ID settings to set this up.

Create iPhone Email

- *Add your email accounts* - Whether you utilize Mail, Perspective, or something similar to Sparrow, you'll want to include your email accounts immediately. For Apple's Email app, touch *Configurations > Accounts & Passwords, then tap Add Accounts.* Choose your email supplier and follow the steps to enter all the knowledge required.

- *See more email preview* - Email lets you start to see the content of a note without starting it. May as well see as a lot of it as you possibly can, right? Utilize Settings > Email and tap on the Preview button. Change your configurations to five lines and get more information from your email messages and never have to get them open up.

- *Established your default accounts* - For reasons

unknown, our iOS Email settings always appear to default to a merchant account we never use, like *iCloud*. Tap *Configurations* > *Accounts & Passwords* > *Your email accounts name, and then touch Accounts* > *Email.* Once you reach the depths of the settings, you can touch your preferred email; this would be your address in new mails. (When there is only one address in here, you're all set.) That is also the spot to add some other email addresses associated with your email account.

Advanced iPhone Email tweaks

- *Swipe to control email* - It's much more helpful to have the ability to swipe your email messages away rather than clicking through and tapping on several control keys. Swipe to Archive, so that whenever you swipe that path, you'll have the ability to either quickly save a contact to your Archive. Or, if your email accounts support swiping left as a default Delete action, it'll offer a Garbage icon. Swipe left to Tag as Read, which is a smart way to slam through your electronic mails as you have them. This only impacts your built-in Email application from Apple. Each third-party email customer can do things differently.

- *Add an HTML signature* - A sound email signature really can cause you to look professional, so make sure to include an HTML signature to your email. If you've already got one on the desktop, duplicate and paste the code into contact and ahead to yourself.

You'll be able to copy and paste it into an Email application (or whichever email supplier you like, if it facilitates it). It could be as easy as textual content formatting tags or as complicated as adding a logo design from a webserver. You should use an iOS application to make one, too; however, they tend to look fairly basic.

Manage Calendars, iCloud, Communications and more

- *Set default Calendar alert times* - Calendar is ideal for alerting you to important occasions, but it's not necessarily at a convenient or useful time. Established the default timing on three types of occasions: Birthdays, Occasions, and All-Day Occasions, and that means you get reminders when they're helpful. Utilize *Configurations > Calendars*. Tap on Default Alert Times and set your Birthday reminders to 1 day before, your Occasions to quarter-hour before (or a period which makes more sense to your mind), and All-Day Occasions on the day of the function (10 a.m.). You'll never miss a meeting again.

- *Background application refresh* - You'll desire to be selective about which applications you desire to be in a position to run in the background, so have a look at the list in *Settings > General >*

Background App Refresh. Toggle Background App Refresh to ON, then toggle OFF all the applications you don't need being able to access anything in the background. When in question, toggle it to OFF and find out if you are slowed up by any applications that require to refresh when you release them. You'll want to allow Background Refresh for Cult of Macintosh Magazine!

Secure Your Web Experience

- *Browser set up* - Surfing the net is filled with forms to complete. Adding your name, address, email, and bank cards may take up a great deal of your power. Make sure to head into Configurations > Browser > AutoFill to create your mobile internet browser the proper way. First, toggle Use Contact Info to On. Then tap on My Info and select the contact you want to use when you encounter form areas in Browser. Toggle Titles and Passwords on as well, and that means you can save that across appointments to the same website. (This pulls from *iCloud Keychain*, so make sure to have that allowed, too.)

Toggle *CREDIT CARDS* to ON as well, which means you can shop swiftly. (*be sure only to use SSL-encrypted websites.*)

Pro suggestion: Manage which bank cards your iPhone helps you to save with a tap on BANK CARDS. You can include new cards within, or delete ones that no more work or that you don't want to use via mobile Browser.

The browser in iOS 13 and later version also blocks cross-site monitoring, which are those cookies that follow you around and let online stores place the same advertisements on every subsequent web page you visit. That is On by default, and that means you should not do anything. Just relax and revel in your newfound personal privacy.

iCloud Everywhere

- *iCloud is everything* - There's without a doubt in

our thoughts that iCloud is the easiest, optimum solution for keeping all of your stuff supported and safe. Utilize the Configurations > iCloud and be sure to register with your **Apple ID**. You can manage your storage space in here, but make sure to enable all you need immediately. Enable iCloud Drive, Photos, Connections, Reminders, Browser, Records, News, Wallet, Back-up, Keychain and others once you get the iPhone unpacked. You can enable Email and Calendars if you merely use Apple's applications and services; usually, you would keep those toggled OFF.

Services subscription during iPhone setup

- *Enable iCloud Photo Library* - We love the iCloud Photo Library. It maintains your photos and videos securely stored in the cloud and enable you to get full-quality copies of your documents in the event you misplace your originals. iCloud Picture Library depends on your iCloud storage space, if you have a lot of photos, you'll want to bump that up. Utilize Configurations > iCloud > Photos, then toggle iCloud Image Library to On. (Remember that this will switch off My Picture Stream. If you'd like both, you'll need to re-toggle Image Stream back again to On.)

- *Use iTunes Match* - Sure, Apple Music monitors all the music data files on your devices, but if you delete them from your iPhone and don't have a back-up elsewhere, you're heading to have to stay for whatever quality Apple Music will provide you with when you listen. If you wish to maintain your full-resolution music documents supported to the cloud, use iTunes Match.

You get all of your music files matched up or published to iCloud in the best bitrate possible. After that, you can stream or download the music to any device provided your iTunes Match membership is intact. Never be without your music (or have an over-filled iPhone) again. Go to *Configurations* > *Music*. Then touch on Sign up to iTunes Match to understand this valuable service allowed on your brand-new iPhone.

More iPhone set up Tweaks

- *Extend your Auto-Lock* - Let's face it. The default two minutes you get for the Volume of time your iPhone would remain on without turning off its screen may keep the battery higher much longer, but it's insufficient for anybody during regular use. Utilize Configurations, General, Auto-Lock to create this to the whole five minutes, which means you can stop tapping your screen at all times to keep it awake.

- *Get texts everywhere* - You can enable your Mac PC or iPad to get texts from your iPhone, provided you've set up iMessage to them (Settings, Text messages, toggle iMessage to ON on any iOS device, Messages Preferences on your Mac). Ensure that your other device is close by when you Utilize Settings on your iPhone, then touch Messages > TEXT Forwarding. Any devices available will arrive on the list. Toggle your Mac or iPad to On, and then check the prospective device for a code. Enter that code into your iPhone. Now all of your devices are certain to get not only iMessages but also texts from those not using iMessage.

- *Equalise your tunes* - Start the EQ in your Music application to be able to hear your preferred jams and never have trouble with a Bluetooth speaker. Go to Configurations > Music. Once there, touch on EQ and established your iPhone to NIGHT TIME; this will provide you with a great quantity rise for those times where you want to blast *The Clash* while you make a quick supper in the kitchen.

Chapter 4

Comprehensive iPhone 11 Features

1. *Six New Gorgeous Colours*

The brand new iPhone 11 would come in six beautiful new colours; they're a little more in the pastel-colour range; however, they look quite right. The colours are *Crimson, White, Green, Yellowish, Dark, and Red.*

2. *Anodised Aluminium and 3D Cup Design*

As you can tell by looking at the back, the iPhone 11 has a fresh design at the end. The iPhone 11 shell is manufactured out of anodized aluminum, and on both edges, there's glass -panel. iPhone 11 includes a 3D cup design that seamlessly merges with the lightweight aluminum band.

3. *A13 Bionic Chip*

Apple says that the 7mm+ based *A13 Bionic chip* gets the fastest CPU in virtually any smartphone. It is up to 20% faster than the CPU inside the A12 chip. The A13 chip has special improvements for machine learning accelerators that permit the CPU to provide more than 1 trillion procedures per second.

4. *Fastest Smartphone GPU in the World*

Apple also says that the iPhone 11 gets the quickest GPU in virtually any smartphone in the marketplace. It's up to 20% faster than the GPU in iPhone XR while also being more power-efficient.

5. *New Main Camera*

The primary camera on the iPhone 11 has been updated; the 12MP sensor has 100% Concentrate Pixels for three times faster autofocus in low light.

6. *New Ultra Wide Camera*

The iPhone 11 gets an entirely new camera, and it's an ultra-wide sensor with a 120-level wide field of view; the 12MP Ultra Wide sensor has an f/2.4 aperture. It gives you to zoom out by 0.5x from the standard shot. By using this camera, you may take some fantastic cinematic shots with an entirely new perspective.

7. *4K Video on Ultra-Wide Camera*

The 4K recording works on the Ultra-Wide camera as well, and you may seamlessly switch between your cameras while shooting the video. You can tap on the move button to focus out, or you can split on the icon to slowly switch between your camera.

8. *Audio Zoom*

The Ultra-Wide camera and the new zoom technology includes an excellent addition in the program. As you move in and out of a video, the sound zooms too!

9. *Night Setting in Camera App*

iPhone 11 has a new low-light setting that converts on automatically and works with no flash. It requires multiple images, while optical image stabilization steadies the zoom lens. Then your software aligns the images with improving for movement and removes sections with too much blur. After that, it de-sounds and enhances all the available details. What you finish up with is your final image using which you can use as it is a lot brighter.

10. *QuickTake*

QuickTake is a fresh feature approaching later in the entire year that enables you to shoot videos while you're taking photos. What's incredible is that it'll keep carefully the same frame and everything the image settings, seamlessly switching to the video mode.

That is something that's not quick to do right now. After the feature boats, all you have to do is touch and hang on the Shutter button to begin recording a video. After that, you can swipe left to lock the video if you want to capture longer videos.

11. *12MP Front side Facing Camera*

There's a new and improved camera sensor in the TrueDepth camera system. It's now a 12MP sensor with an f/2.2 aperture.

12. *Faster Face Identification with Greater Angles*

Face ID is currently 30% faster, and it works at higher perspectives. So even if the telephone is in a roundabout way looking at you right in the facial skin, Face Identification unlock will still work.

13. *Slo-mo on Front side Facing Camera*

Apple wants to make selfies something. Now you can catch slow-motion video from the front-facing camera at up to 120 fps.

14. *4K Documenting on Front side Facing Camera*

Plus, you can record 4K video on the front-facing camera at 24, 30, or 60 fps.

15. *Portrait Setting Works together with Pets*

Thanks to the way the new wide and ultra-wide cameras interact, the portrait mode on the iPhone 11 now works for pets too! That is something we've wanted since Apple launched the iPhone XR this past year with Portrait mode but limited it only to humans.

16. *Spatial Sound with Dolby Atmos*

The speakers in the iPhone 11 include 3D Spatial sound technology. It simulates audio for a far more immersive experience; the brand new iPhone also comes with Dolby Atmos' support.

17. *Deep Fusion*

Deep Fusion is a new image control technology by Apple that will dispatch with a software update later in the Fall. It's another form of image structure technology. Apple requires four primary and four additional photos before you press the shutter button. When you press the shutter button, it requires one huge publicity picture to get as much fine detail as possible.

After that, it works pixel-by-pixel to stitch the facts collectively from all the photos in the best manner. Everything you get can be an image with an incredible level of detail.

18. *Longer Electric battery Life than iPhone XR*

iPhone XR already had a fantastic all-day electric battery

life. iPhone 11 pushes the pub further with the addition of a complete hour to the electronic battery life. That's up to 17 hours of video playback or more to 10 hours of video loading time.

19. *New U1 Chip*

iPhone 11 has an entirely new chip called U1 that uses Ultra-Wideband technology for spacial consciousness; this enables iPhone 11 to locate other U1 devices precisely. If you wish to share a document using AirDrop, point your iPhone at theirs, and they'll be the first in the set of the AirDrop posting screen.

20. *Toughest Cup Ever in a Smartphone*

Apple has heard your issues loud and clear. Having a back again design that is accurately milled and sculpted from an individual piece of a cup, iPhone 11 features the most robust cup ever in a smartphone; this will help protect your iPhone in the event when it drops.

21. *Improved Water-Resistance*

iPhone 11 is IP68 certified; this implies it can withstand up to 2 meters of drinking water for thirty minutes.

22. *Extended Active Range*

The extended active range feature on the iPhone 11 while

documenting videos is currently designed for 4k videos at up to 60fps. Around the iPhone XR, this is limited by 30fps videos only.

23. *Gigabit-class LTE*

iPhone 11 features Gigabit-class LTE that may help you get the best rates of speed on your moves; this is a significant omission on the iPhone XR, so it's nice to see Apple finally making your way around to adding it.

24. *Wi-Fi 6*

iPhone 11 is the first new iPhone to aid the new Wi-Fi 6 standard for faster download rates of speed. Apart from this, the iPhone 11 has yet featured that you found in iPhone XR. So that it still supports cellular charging, fast charging with the optionally available 18-watt charger that should be bought individually, Dual SIM support with eSIM, and more.

iPhone 11 will dispatch with iOS 13, with support for editing and enhancing 4K videos, dark setting, and many more.

CHAPTER 5

Restoring iPhone 11 Backup from iCloud and iTunes

There is no need connecting your brand-new iPhone 11 Series (iPhone 11, iPhone 11 Pro, and iPhone 11 Pro Max) to your personal computer, as long as there is a mobile data connection designed for activation. As you end the set-up wizard, you may navigate back by tapping the back arrow at the top left-hand side of the screen and scroll further to another display by tapping another button at the top right-hand corner.

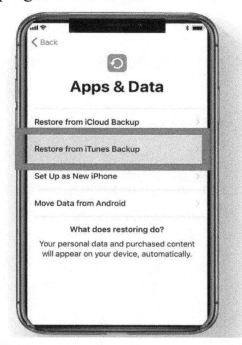

You can commence by pressing down the power button at the top edge of your brand-new iPhone 11 Series (iPhone 11, iPhone 11 Pro and iPhone 11 Pro Max). You may want to keep it pressed down for about two seconds until you notice a vibration, meaning the iPhone 11 Series (iPhone 11, iPhone 11 Pro and iPhone 11 Pro Max) is booting up.

Once it boots up finally, you can start initial set up by following the processes below;

- Swipe your finger over the display screen to start the set-up wizard.
- Choose the language of preference - English is usually at the top of the list, so there is no problem finding it. However, if you would like to apply a different language, scroll down to look for your desired *language*, and tap to select the preferred language.
- Choose your *country* - the *United States,* for instance, which may be close to the top of the list. If otherwise, scroll down the list and select the

United States or any of your choice.

- You need to connect your iPhone 11 Series (iPhone 11, iPhone 11 Pro, and iPhone 11 Pro Max) to the internet to start its activation. You can test this via a link with a Wi-Fi network. Locate the name of your available network in the list shown, and then tap on it to select it.

- Enter the Wi-Fi security password (you will generally find this written on your router, which is probably known as the WPA Key, WEP Key, or Password) and select Sign up. A tick indication shows you are connected, and a radio image appears near the top of the screen. The iPhone 11 Series (iPhone 11, iPhone 11 Pro, and iPhone 11 Pro Max) would now start activation with Apple automatically. It may take some time!

- In case your iPhone 11 Series (iPhone 11, iPhone 11 Pro, and iPhone 11 Pro Max) is a 4G version, you would be requested to check for updated internet configurations after inserting a new Sim card. You can test this anytime, so, for the present time, tap **Continue**.

- Location services would help you with mapping, weather applications, and more, giving you specific information centred wholly on what your location is. Select whether to use location service by tapping allow location services.

- You would now be requested to create **Touch ID,** which is Apple's fingerprint identification. **Touch ID** allows you to unlock your iPhone 11 Series (iPhone 11, iPhone 11 Pro, and iPhone 11 Pro Max) with your fingerprint instead of your passcode or security password. To set up Tap Identification, put a finger or your thumb on the home button (but do not press it down!). To by-pass this for the moment, tap *setup Touch ID later*.

- If you are establishing Touch ID, the tutorial instruction on the screen will walk you through the set-up process. Put your finger on the home button, then remove it till the iPhone 11 Series (iPhone 11, iPhone 11 Pro, and iPhone 11 Pro Max) has properly scanned your fingerprint. Whenever your print is wholly scanned, you would notice a screen letting you know that tap recognition is successful.

Tap **Continue**.

- You would be requested to enter a passcode to secure your iPhone 11 Series (iPhone 11, iPhone 11 Pro, and iPhone 11 Pro Max). If you create **Touch ID**, you must use a passcode if, in any case, your fingerprint isn't acknowledged. Securing your computer data is an excellent idea, and the iPhone 11 Series (iPhone 11, iPhone 11 Pro, and iPhone 11 Pro Max) provides you with several options. Tap password option to choose your lock method.

- You can arrange a Custom Alphanumeric Code (that is a security password that uses characters and figures), a Custom Numeric Code (digit mainly useful, however, you can add as many numbers as you want!) or a 4-Digit Numeric Code. In case you didn't install or set up **Touch ID,** you may even have an option not to add a Security password. Tap on your selected Security option.

- I would recommend establishing a 4-digit numeric code, or Touch ID for security reasons, but all optional setup is done likewise. Input your selected Security password using the keyboard.

- Verify your Security password by inputting it again. If the Password does not match, you'll be requested to repeat! If indeed they do match, you'll continue to another display automatically.

At this time of the set-up process, you'll be asked whether you have used an iPhone 11 Series (iPhone 11, iPhone 11 Pro and iPhone 11 Pro Max) before and probably upgrading it, you can restore all of your applications and information from an iCloud or iTunes backup by deciding on the best option. If this is your first iPhone 11 Series (iPhone 11, iPhone 11 Pro and iPhone 11 Pro Max), you would have to get it started as new, yet, in case you are moving from Android to an iPhone 11 Series (iPhone 11, iPhone 11 Pro and iPhone 11 Pro Max), you can transfer all your data by deciding and choosing the choice you want.

How to Move Data From an Android Phone

Apple has made it quite easy to move your data from a Google Android device to your new iPhone 11 Series (iPhone 11, iPhone 11 Pro and iPhone 11 Pro Max).

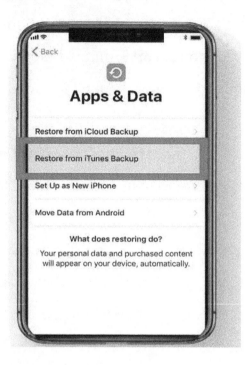

Proceed to the iOS app. I'll direct you about how to use the application to move your data!

- Using the iPhone 11 Series (iPhone 11, iPhone 11 Pro and iPhone 11 Pro Max), if you are on the applications & data screen of the set-up wizard, tap *move data from Google android*.

- Go to the Play Store on your Google android device and download the app recommended by the set-up wizard. When it is installed, open up the app, select **Continue,** and you'll be shown the *Terms &*

Conditions to continue.

- On your Android device, tap *Next* to start linking your Devices. On your own iPhone 11 Series (iPhone 11, iPhone 11 Pro, and iPhone 11 Pro Max), select *Continue*.

- Your iPhone 11 Series (iPhone 11, iPhone 11 Pro, and iPhone 11 Pro Max) would show a 6-digit code that has to be received into the **Google android** device to set the two phones up.

- Your Google android device would screen all the data that'll be moved. By default, all options are ticked - so if there could be something you don't want to move, tap the related collection to deselect it. If you are prepared to continue, tap *Next* on your Google android device.

- As the change progresses, you would notice the iPhone 11 Series (iPhone 11, iPhone 11 Pro, and iPhone 11 Pro Max) display screen changes, showing you the position of the info transfer and progress report.

- When the transfer is completed, you will notice a confirmation screen on each device. On your

Android Device, select ***Done*** to shut the app. On your own iPhone 11 Series (iPhone 11, iPhone 11 Pro, and iPhone 11 Pro Max), tap ***Continue***.

- An ***Apple ID*** allows you to download apps, supported by your iPhone 11 Series and synchronize data through multiple devices, which makes it an essential account you should have on your iPhone 11 Series! If you have been using an iPhone X phones previously, or use iTunes to download music to your laptop, then you should have already become an *Apple ID* user. Register with your username and passwords (when you have lost or forgotten your Apple ID or password, you will see a link that may help you reset it). If you're not used to iPhone 11 Series (iPhone 11, iPhone 11 Pro and iPhone 11 Pro Max), select doesn't have an Apple ID to create one for free.

- The Terms & Conditions for your iPhone 11 Series (iPhone 11, iPhone 11 Pro and iPhone 11 Pro Max) can be seen. Please go through them (tapping on more to study additional info), so when you are done, tap ***Agree***.

- You'll be asked about synchronizing your data with iCloud. That's to ensure bookmarks, connections, and other items of data are supported securely with your other iPhone 11 Series (iPhone 11, iPhone 11 Pro, and iPhone 11 Pro Max)'s data. Tap *merge* to permit this or ***don't merge*** if you'll have a choice to keep your details elsewhere asides iCloud.

- **Apple pay** is Apple's secure payment system that stores encrypted credit or debit card data on your device and making use of your iPhone 11 Series (iPhone 11, iPhone 11 Pro, and iPhone 11 Pro Max) also with your fingerprint to make safe transactions online and with other apps. Select *Next* to continue.

- To *feature/add a card*, place it on a set surface and place the iPhone 11 Series (iPhone 11, iPhone 11 Pro, and iPhone 11 Pro Max) over it, so the card is put in the camera framework. The credit card info would be scanned automatically, and you would be requested to verify that the details on display correspond with your card. You'll also be asked to enter the *CVV* (safety code) from the personal strip behind the card. If you choose (or the camera cannot recognize your cards), you can enter credit card information by hand by tapping the hyperlink. You could bypass establishing **Apple Pay** by tapping *create later*.

- Another screen discusses the *iCloud keychain*, which is Apple's secure approach to sharing your preserved security password and payment information throughout all your Apple devices. You might use *iCloud security code* to validate your brand-new device and import present data, or you might be asked to continue registering your keychain if it's your first Apple device. In case you don't want to share vital data with other devices, you should go to *avoid iCloud keychain* or *don't restore passwords*.

- If you want to set up your Apple keychain, you'd be notified to either use a Security password (the same one you'd set up on your iPhone 11 Series (iPhone 11, iPhone 11 Pro, and iPhone 11 Pro Max)) or produce a different code. If you're making use of your iCloud security code, you should put it on your iPhone 11 Series (iPhone 11, iPhone 11 Pro, and iPhone 11 Pro Max) when prompted.

- This would confirm your ID when signing on to an iCloud safety code; a confirmation code would be delivered via SMS. You may want to hyperlink your smartphone text code (if you have never distributed one with Apple already) so that the code may be provided as a text. Then enter this code to your iPhone 11 Series (iPhone 11, iPhone 11 Pro, and iPhone 11 Pro Max) if requested, then select *Next.*

- You'll then be asked to create **Siri**. *Siri* is your own digital personal associate, which might search the internet, send communications, and check out data in your device and a lot more, all without having to flick via specific apps. Choose to create Siri by tapping the choice or start Siri later to skip this task for now.

- To set up and create SIRI, you would need to speak several phrases to the iPhone 11 Series (iPhone 11, iPhone 11 Pro, and iPhone 11 Pro Max) to review your conversation patterns and identify your voice.

- Once you say every term, a tick would be observed, showing that it's been known and comprehended. Another phrase may indicate that you should read aloud.

- Once you've completed the five phrases, you would notice a display notifying that Siri has been set up correctly. Tap *Continue*.

- The iPhone 11 Series (iPhone 11, iPhone 11 Pro, and iPhone 11 Pro Max) display alters the colour balance to help make the screen show up naturally under distinctive light conditions. You can switch this off in the screen settings after the iPhone 11 Series (iPhone 11, iPhone 11 Pro, and iPhone 11 Pro Max) has completed configuring it. Tap *continue* to continue with the setup.

- Has your iPhone 11 Series (iPhone 11, iPhone 11 Pro, and iPhone 11 Pro Max) been restored? Tap begin to transfer your computer data to your brand-new iPhone 11 Series (iPhone 11, iPhone 11 Pro, and iPhone 11 Pro Max).

- You'll be prompted to ensure your brand-new iPhone 11 Series (iPhone 11, iPhone 11 Pro and iPhone 11 Pro Max) has enough power to avoid the device turning off in the process of downloading applications and information. Tap *OK* to verify this recommendation.

- You would notice a notification show up on your apps to download in the background.

NB: Setting up any new iPhone model: A similar method, as described above, applies.

How to Restore iPhone 11 Back-up from iCloud or iTunes

If you want to restore your iPhone 11 Series (iPhone 11, iPhone 11 Pro, and iPhone 11 Pro Max) from an iTunes back-up, you may want to connect to iCloud and have the latest version of iTunes installed on it. If you are ready to begin this process, tap **restore** from iTunes back-up on your iPhone 11 Series and connect it to your personal computer. Instructions about how to bring back your data can be followed on the laptop screen.

In case your old iPhone model was supported on iCloud, then follow the instructions below to restore your applications & data to your brand-new device:

- Tap *Restore* from iCloud back-up.
- Register with the Apple ID and Password that you applied to your old iPhone. If you fail to recollect the security password, there's a link that may help you reset it.
- The Terms & Conditions screen would show. Tap the links to learn about specific areas in detail.

When you are ready to proceed, select **Agree**.

- Your iPhone 11 Series (iPhone 11, iPhone 11 Pro, and iPhone 11 Pro Max) would need some moments to create your Apple ID and hook up with the iCloud server.

- You would notice a summary of available backups to download. The most up-to-date backup would be observed at the very top, with almost every other option below it. If you want to restore from a desirable backup, tap the screen for *all backups* to see the available choices.

- Tap on the back-up you want to restore to start installing.

- A progress bar would be shown, providing you with a demo of the advancement of the download. When the restore is completed, the device will restart.

- You would see a notification telling you that your iPhone 11 Series (iPhone 11, iPhone 11 Pro, and iPhone 11 Pro Max) is updated effectively. Tap *Continue*.

- To complete the iCloud set up on your recently

restored iPhone 11 Series (iPhone 11, iPhone 11 Pro, and iPhone 11 Pro Max), you should re-enter your iCloud (Apple ID) password. Enter/review it and then tap *Next*.

- You'll be prompted to upgrade the security information related to your ***Apple ID***. Tap on any stage to replace your computer data, or even to bypass this option. If you aren't ready to do this, then tap the *Next* button.

- **Apple pay** is Apple's secure payment system that stores encrypted credit or debit card data on your device and making use of your iPhone 11 Series (iPhone 11, iPhone 11 Pro, and iPhone 11 Pro Max) also with your fingerprint to make safe transactions online and with other apps. Select *Next* to continue.

- To *feature/add a card*, place it on a set surface and place the iPhone 11 Series (iPhone 11, iPhone 11 Pro, and iPhone 11 Pro Max) over it, so the card is put in the camera framework. The credit card info would be scanned automatically, and you would be requested to verify that the details on display correspond with your card. You'll also be asked to enter the *CVV* (safety code) from the personal strip behind the card. If you choose (or the camera cannot recognize your cards), you can enter credit card information by hand by tapping the hyperlink. You could bypass establishing **Apple Pay** by tapping *create later*.

- Another screen discusses the *iCloud keychain*, which is Apple's secure approach to sharing your preserved security password and payment information throughout all your Apple devices. You might use *iCloud security code* to validate your brand-new device and import present data, or you might be asked to continue registering your keychain if it's your first Apple device. In case you don't want to share vital data with other devices, you should go to *avoid iCloud keychain* or *don't restore passwords*.

- If you selected to set up your Apple keychain, you'd be notified to either uses a Security password (the same one you'd set up on your iPhone 11 Series (iPhone 11, iPhone 11 Pro and iPhone 11

Pro Max)) or provide a different code. If you're making use of your iCloud security code, you should put it on your iPhone 11 Series (iPhone 11, iPhone 11 Pro, and iPhone 11 Pro Max) when prompted.

- This would confirm your ID when signing on to an iCloud safety code; a confirmation code would be delivered via SMS. You may want to hyperlink your smartphone text code (if you have never distributed one with Apple already) so that the code may be provided as a text. Then enter this code to your iPhone 11 Series (iPhone 11, iPhone 11 Pro, and iPhone 11 Pro Max) if requested, then select *Next.*

- You'll then be asked to create **Siri**. *Siri* is your own digital personal associate, which might search the internet, send communications, and check out data in your device and a lot more, all without having to flick via specific apps. Choose to create Siri by tapping the choice or start Siri later to skip this task for now.

- To set up and create SIRI, you would need to

speak several phrases to the iPhone 11 Series (iPhone 11, iPhone 11 Pro, and iPhone 11 Pro Max) to review your conversation patterns and identify your voice.

- Once you say every term, a tick would be observed, showing that it's been known and comprehended. Another phrase may indicate that you should read aloud.

- Once you've completed the five phrases, you would notice a display notifying that Siri has been set up correctly. Tap *Continue*.

- The iPhone 11 Series (iPhone 11, iPhone 11 Pro, and iPhone 11 Pro Max) display alters the colour balance to help make the screen show up naturally under distinctive light conditions. You can switch this off in the screen settings after the iPhone 11 Series (iPhone 11, iPhone 11 Pro, and iPhone 11 Pro Max) has completed configuring it. Tap *continue* to continue with the setup.

- Has your iPhone been restored? Tap begin to transfer your computer data to your brand-new iPhone 11 Series (iPhone 11, iPhone 11 Pro, and iPhone 11 Pro Max).

- You'll be prompted to ensure your brand-new iPhone 11 Series (iPhone 11, iPhone 11 Pro and iPhone 11 Pro Max) has enough charge to avoid the device turning off in the process of downloading applications and information. Tap *OK* to verify this recommendation.
- You would notice a notification show up on your apps to download in the background.

Chapter 6

iPhone 11 Guidelines: How to unlock its Photographic Potential

Taking photos in the iPhone's default camera application is pretty simple and straightforward - in fact, almost too simple for individuals who need to get a little more creative using their shots. Well, that's all transformed on the iPhone 11 and iPhone 11 Pro, which not only brings a fresh wide-angle zoom lens but a pleasant assisting of new software features that you should explore.

The difficulty is, a few of these aren't immediately apparent, and it's not necessarily clear just how to take benefit of the excess photographic power stored in your shiny new iPhone.

That's why we've come up with this beginner guide for the iPhone 11 and iPhone 11 Pro's digital cameras, to get a solid foothold and springtime towards Instagram greatness. Continue reading and get snapping.

1. *Figure out how to look beyond your frame*

When shooting the typical (26mm comparative) zoom lens, the iPhone 11 and iPhone 11 Pro use the wide-angle zoom lens showing you what's happening beyond your frame, a little just like a range-finder camera. Those digital cameras have always been popular with professional road photographers because they enable you to nail the precise moment when a fascinating character walks into the frame.

You shouldn't do anything to create this up - endure your iPhone 11 with the camera application open and point it towards the scene to view it in action. Look for a photogenic background like a vacant road, then use the wide-angle preview to time as soon as your subject matter enters the shot. Want to keep the wide-angle view of your picture carefully.

2. *Adjust your compositions*

Here's another fun new feature on the iPhone 11 and iPhone 11 Pro that's great if you can't quite determine the ultimate way to take a picture. You'll need to go to the main configurations, wherein the Camera section; you'll find an option called "*Composition.*" If you enable "Photos Catch Outside the Framework," the camera will record two photos at the same time - one using the wide-angle zoom lens, and another using the typical angle.

There are always a few facts to consider when working with this nifty trick. First is that you'll have to take in the HEIF format, which isn't always dealt with well by non-iOS devices. Also, the broader position picture will be erased if it's not used within thirty days, so you'll have to be reasonably quick with your editing and enhancing.

To get the wide-angle view of the shot, tap *'Edit'* within the photo, then your cropping icon, then press the three dots button in the very best right and choose "Use Content Beyond your Frame."

3. *Manage HDR*

The iPhone 11 and iPhone 11 Pro include Smart HDR, which is started up by default; this automatically detects the light levels in your picture and protect both shows and shadows for a far more balanced image.

More often than not, you will see occasions when challenging conditions lead to a graphic, which is nearly right. If you'd favour less processed photos to edit within an application like Lightroom, check out the configurations menu, find the Camera section, then switch off Smart HDR.

The great thing concerning this is it doesn't eliminate using Smart HDR for several scenes - in the Camera application, you'll now see an HDR button at the very top to turn it On/Off. It just means your default capturing will be without Smart HDR's sometimes overzealous processing.

4. *Reach grips with Night Mode*

Night mode is a new feature for the iPhone 11 and iPhone 11 Pro - and it's something we've been waiting around to see in a while. It's not an ardent setting you can opt for - instead, it'll activate automatically when the iPhone detects that ambient light conditions are on the reduced side.

Nevertheless, you can still have little control over it once it is used; tap the night time setting icon at the left, and you may use a split to choose a faster shutter speed if it's brighter than the telephone realizes, or leave it on Car - or you can also choose to turn it off entirely carefully.

It's worth keeping your iPhone 11 constant on the surface, or perhaps a tripod if you have one, as the telephone will recognize this and raise the shutter rate to 30 mere seconds, which is potentially ideal for night sky photos.

5. *Grasp the ultra-wide-angle lens*

The iPhone 11 and iPhone 11 Pro will be the first ones with a super wide-angle lens. If you haven't used one before, their 13mm equivalent field of view will come in super-handy for several different subjects, but particularly landscape and architecture, where you want to fit in as much of the scene as possible.

If you wish to exceed dramatic building pictures, one common technique utilized by professional scenery photographers is to juxtapose one close object with a distant object - for example, some close by plants with a long way background subject.

You could also want to use it in a while composing in portrait orientation, for a fascinating new look that wouldn't have been possible before with older iPhones.

6. *Portrait setting is not only for humans*

Even though iPhone XR had a great camera, you couldn't use the inbuilt Family portrait mode for anything apart from human subjects. Bad information for pet-lovers, or merely those who wish to create a shallow depth of field results with any subject.

That's all transformed for the iPhone 11, which uses its two digital cameras to help you to take shallow depth-of-field impact images for many different subjects, and has been specially optimised for domestic pets. To begin with, all you have to do is swipe to *Family portrait mode* and point the camera the four-legged friend. It'll tell you if you're too near to the subject and instruct you to move away. The details are nearly perfect, but they're perfect - particularly if you're looking on a little screen.

7. *Locate those lacking settings*

Through the keynote release of the iPhone 11 and iPhone 11 Pro, it was announced that the native camera application would be simplified to help you consider the key method of shooting your images.

That's great and produces a much cleaner interface, but it can imply that some configurations are now just a little concealed away. If you think where they've eliminated, touch the arrow near the top of the display, and you'll find a range of different alternatives, including aspect percentage (see below), adobe flash, night setting (if it's dark enough), timer and digital filter systems.

8. *Try the new 16:9 aspect ratio*

This is an attribute that is new for the iPhone 11 and iPhone 11 Pro, adding a new aspect ratio to the prevailing 4:3 and square (1:1) options. Using a 16:9 aspect percentage is ways to get more full shots which ingest more of the scene, and also eventually screen very nicely on the iPhone display screen.

You'll need to activate it from the menu - the default is 4:3. It's well worth also using the 16:9 aspect proportion with the ultra-wide position to get some good great breathtaking type shots.

C h a p t e r 7

How to start Dark Setting on your iPhone in iOS 13

First, check out *'Configurations'* and then look for *'Screen & Lighting.'* Once there, you'll see an all-new interface that places dark setting front side and centre. You will toggle between *'Light'* and *'Dark'* mode with only a tap, assuming you want to activate it manually; however, its implementation within iOS is just a little smarter than either 'on' or 'off.'

Under the two main options, you'll also visit a toggle marked *'Automatic'* which, as you may be able to think, switches dark setting on alone, linked with sunset and sunrise. Additionally, you then have the choice to define specific times for dark settings to allow and disable.

Dark mode has shown to be one of the very most hyped features approaching to cellular devices in 2019. It isn't just a capability destined for iOS 13 either, it's a significant feature in Google android ten plus some devices have previously instigated their own undertake dark setting - cell phones like the Asus ZenFone 6 and the OnePlus 7 Pro.

What does Dark Mode in iOS 13 do?

A part of dark mode's charm originates from the decrease in power usage it brings, particularly on devices that use OLED shows, like the iPhone X, XS, and XS Maximum. Beyond power intake, however, darker interface shades also lessen eye strain, particularly when being viewed in dark surroundings. In some cases, alternative UI and font colours are also associated with alleviating conditions like Scotopic Level of sensitivity Syndrome - an affliction commonly within people that have dyslexia, which makes text visibility and comprehension difficult.

How to Upgrade Applications on your iPhone in iOS 13

If you're used to manually updating your applications on either an iPhone, iPad or iPod touch by going to the updates tabs in the App Store, then iOS 13 has made some changes. That tabs has eliminated and has been changed by *Arcade*. If you don't anticipate using the new Apple Arcade membership video gaming service, then there's no chance to eliminate this.

Here's how to revise your applications in iOS 13:

- Start the App Store on your iPhone.

- Tap the round consumer icon at the right-hand corner.

- Scroll down, and you'll see a list of all of your applications that either have updates available or have been recently updated.

- If an application comes with an update available, you can hit the button to start it manually

Do applications automatically upgrade in iOS 13?

It appears clear that the reason behind Apple moving this program is because applications tend to update themselves quietly in the background, removing the necessity for anybody to manage application updates manually. The downside with this is that it could be challenging to learn what new features have found its way to applications if you're not looking at the release notes.

Chapter 8

How to Customize Your iPhone Mobile

Customize iPhone Ringtones & Text message Tones

The ringtones and text tones your iPhone uses to get your attention need not be exactly like everyone else's. You may make all types of changes, including changing the sound, and that means you know who's phoning or texting without even taking a glance at your phone.

- *Change the Default Ringtone*: Your iPhone comes pre-loaded with a large number of ringtones. Change the default ringtone for all those calls to the main one you prefer the better to get notified when you experience a call to arrive. Do this by *heading to Settings -> Noises (Noises & Haptics on some models) -> Ringtone.*

- *Set Person Ringtones*: You can assign a different ringtone for everybody in your connections list. That way, a love track can play whenever your partner calls, and you know it's them before even looking. Do that by heading to *Phone -> Connections -> tapping the individual whose ringtone you want to improve -> Edit -> Ringtone.*

- *Get Full-Screen Photos for Incoming Phone calls*: The incoming call screen does not have to be boring. With this suggestion, you can view a fullscreen picture of the individual calling you. Go to *Mobile phone -> Connections -> touch the individual -> Edit -> Add Picture.*

- ***Customize Text Tone***: Like everyone else can customize the ringtones that play for calls, you can customize the appearance like video when you get texts. Go to *Configurations -> Seems (Noises & Haptics on some models) -> Text message Tone.*

TIPS: You're not limited by the band and text tone that include the iPhone. You can purchase ringtones from Apple, and some applications help you create your tone.

Other iPhone Customisation Options

Here's an assortment of a few other different ways to customize your iPhones.

- ***Delete Pre-Installed Apps***: Got a couple of applications pre-installed on your iPhone you don't use? You can delete them (well, the majority of them, anyhow)! Just use the typical way to delete apps: Touch and keep until they tremble, then tap the x on the application icon.

- ***Customize Control Centre***: Control Centre has a lot more options that are apparent initially.

Customize Control Centre to get just the group of tools you want to use. Head to *Settings -> Control Centre -> Customize Settings.*

- ***Install your preferred Keyboard***: The iPhone includes an excellent onscreen keypad; nevertheless, you can install third-party keyboards that add cool features, like *Google search, emojis, and GIFs, plus much more.* Get yourself a new keyboard at the App Store, then go to *Settings -> General -> Keyboard -> Keyboards.*

- ***Make Siri a friend***: Choose to have Siri talk with you utilizing a man's tone of voice? It could happen. Head to *Settings -> Siri & Search -> Siri Tone of voice -> Male.* You can even go with different accents if you want.

- ***Change Browser's default search engine***: Have search engines apart from Google that you'd like to use? Make it the default for those queries in Browser. Head to *Settings -> Browser -> Search Engine and making a new selection.*

- *Make Your Shortcuts*: If you an iPhone 11 or newer version user, you can create all sorts of cool customized gestures and shortcuts for various jobs.

- *Jailbreak Your Phone*: To get the most control over customizing your mobile phone, you can jailbreak it; this gets rid of Apple's settings over certain types of customization. Jailbreaking can cause functional problems and lessen your phone's security, but it can give more control.

Customize iPhone Home Screen

You may take a look at your iPhone home screen more than some other single screen so that it should be set up the way you want it to appear. Below are a few options for customizing your iPhone home screen.

- *Change Your Wallpaper*: You may make the image behind your applications on the home screen just about whatever you want. A favourite picture of your children or spouse or the logo design of your preferred team is a few options.

Find the wallpaper settings by heading to *Settings -> Wallpaper -> Select a New Wallpaper*.

- ***Use Live or Video Wallpaper***: Want something eye-catching? Use cartoon wallpapers instead. There are a few restrictions, but this is relatively cool. *Head to Settings -> Wallpaper -> Select a New Wallpaper -> pick and choose Active or Live.*

- ***Put Apps into Folders***: Organize your home screen centred on how you Utilize applications by grouping them into folders. Begin by gently tapping and securing one application until all your apps begin to tremble. Then pull and drop one application onto another to place those two applications into a folder.

- ***Add Extra Webpages of Apps***: All your apps won't need to be about the same home screen. You may make individual "webpages" for different kinds of applications or different users by tapping and keeping applications or folders, then dragging them from the right side of the screen. Browse the

"Creating Web pages on iPhone" portion of How to Manage Apps on the iPhone Home Screen to get more.

iPhone Customizations that make things Better to see

It isn't always a simple text message or onscreen items on your iPhone, but these customizations make things much simpler to see.

- *Use Screen Focus*: Do all the onscreen symbols and text message look a little too small for your eye? Screen Move magnifies your iPhone screen automatically. To Utilize this option, go to *Settings -> Screen & Brightness -> View -> Zoomed -> Collection.*

- *Change Font Size*: The default font size on your iPhone may be a little small for your eye; nevertheless, you can raise it to make reading convenient. Head to *Settings -> General -> Availability -> Larger Text message -> move the slider to On/green -> change the slider below.*

- ***Use Dark mode***: If the shiny colours of the iPhone screen strain your eye, you may choose to use Dark Setting, which inverts shiny colours to darker ones. Find the essential Dark settings in *Configurations -> General -> Convenience -> Screen Accommodations -> Invert Colours.*

Customize iPhone Lock Screen

Like everyone else, you can customize your home screen; you can customize the iPhone lock screen, too. In this manner, you have control over the very first thing you see each time you wake up your phone.

- ***Customize Lock Screen Wallpaper***: Exactly like on the home screen, you can transform your iPhone lock screen wallpaper to employ a picture, computer animation, or video. Browse the link within the last section for details.

- ***Create a Stronger Passcode***: The much longer your passcode, the harder it is to break right into your iPhone (you are utilizing a passcode, right?). The default passcode is 4 or 6 character types (depending on your iOS version); nevertheless, you make it much longer and stronger. *Head to Settings -> Face ID (or Touch ID) & Passcode -> Change Passcode and following an instructions.*

- ***Get Suggestions from Siri***: Siri can learn your practices, preferences, passions, and location and then use that information to suggest content for you. Control what Siri suggests by heading to *Configurations -> Siri & Search -> Siri Recommendations and setting the things you want to use to On/green.*

Customize iPhone Notifications

Your iPhone helpfully notifies you to understand when you have calls, text messages, emails, and other bits of information that may interest you. But those notifications can be irritating. Customize how you get notifications with these pointers.

- *Choose Your Notification Style*: The iPhone enables you to choose lots of notification styles, from simple pop-ups to a mixture of sound and text messages, and more. Find the notification options in *Settings -> Notifications -> touch the application you want to regulate -> choose Alerts, Banner Style, Noises, and more.*

- *Group Notifications from the Same App*: Get yourself many notifications from an individual app, but won't need to see each one taking space on your screen? You can group notifications into a *"stack"* that occupies the same space as your notification. Control this on the per-app basis by heading to *Settings -> Notifications -> the application you want to regulate -> Notification Grouping.*

- *Adobe flashes a Light for Notifications*: Unless you want to try out to get a notification, you may make the camera adobe flashlight instead. It's a delicate, but apparent, option for most situations. Set this up in *Settings -> General ->*

Convenience -> Hearing -> move the LED Screen for Notifications slider to On/green.

- ***Get Notification Previews with Face ID***: In case your iPhone has Face ID, you can utilize it to keep the notifications private. This establishing shows a simple headline in notifications; however, when you go through the screen and get identified by Face ID, the notification expands, showing more content. Establish this by going to *Settings -> Notifications -> Show Previews -> When Unlocked.*

TIPS: That link also offers an excellent tips about using Face ID to silent alarms, and notification sounds, i.e., *"Reduce Alarm Volume and Keep Screen Shiny with Attention Awareness."*

- ***Get more information with Notification Centre Widgets***: Notification Centre not only gathers all your notifications, but it also offers up widgets, mini-versions of applications to enable you to do things without starting apps whatsoever.

Chapter 9

5 Ways of Upgrading Your iPhone Digital Photography for Instagram

1. Minimalism is Key

Our number 1 Instagram photography suggestion is to consider photos that look great and professional with your iPhone; you would need to believe. Why? Because it is not only better - but it's much simpler to choose one new subject matter and make that the centre point of your image.

The sure sign of the amateur is a person who tries to match so many subjects to their imagery. "But my image would be filled with vacant space!" you may protest. That's flawlessly fine. Professional photographers call bare space, *'negative space,'* which is another technique which makes your centre point stand out.

The ultimate way to do this is to go closer to the topic and remove anything in the shot that may distract the viewer.

This can make your Instagram photography appear to be like an expert did it. As you keep up to apply this, you'll come to find that minimalism is the most shared on systems like Instagram, because photos with ONE centre point stick out on smartphone screens.

2. **Get low in Position**

Understandably, your camera move shouldn't be filled with selfies. Just as your camera move shouldn't contain images used at chest elevation.

Among the quickest ways to update your Instagram digital photography and create images that stick out is to take from a lesser position than what you're used to. You don't need to get too low either, capture from less than what you're used to.

When you take your subject or centre point from such a minimal angle that the sky is the only background, what you finish up doing is following both Instagram picture taking Tip 1 and Tip 2 - making the image extremely attractive on the system like Instagram.

So when you're finally more comfortable with the thought of looking, "extra" according to some people, you'll be able to start squatting and even kneeling to be able to get the best low-angle images.

3. <u>Depth of Field</u>

Precisely what does *"depth of field"* mean? Blurring backgrounds, of course! Everyone knows an image with blur looks a lot more interesting than a graphic where the background and the foreground are both in concentration.

When you Utilize zoom lens accessories to mention a feeling of depth in your images, i.e. Telephoto lenses, you'll be able to attract people's attention - whether you're photographing accessories for Instagram, or just taking scenery photographs.

Besides getting hold of iPhone accessories, a straightforward technique like using "leading lines" that direct the audiences' focus on whatever it is that has been snapped is a superb way to produce depth for your Instagram digital photography. For instance, going for a picture of the road, railway track, a riverbank, fences, and pathways are an excellent leading line!

Once you have found your leads, you can create some depth in the foreground by using found items like stones or leaves or other things, for example, When you absolutely cannot find anything in the foreground that could add a component appealing, then get back to Suggestion #2 and "Get Low in position"! Take from a lesser angle, and you will be amazed what you can catch.

4. Get Up-Close and Personal

Okay, so right now, you've probably determined that each of the tips accumulates from the prior tips so that by enough time you've mastered this whole list, you're practically an expert!

Your Instagram picture taking needs details! It might be hard to trust, but a great deal of iPhone professional photographers make the error of not getting close enough to the centre point. Particularly when they're photographing something with a great deal of fine detail - i.e. When you capture from a long distance, the picture eventually ends up being a little dull and impersonal; however, when you get near to the thing, you all of a sudden have an image that involves life - particularly when you take portraits of others or even your selfies. When you move nearer to the subject, you can properly catch cosmetic features and feelings that would build relationships with the viewer.

Even the newer iPhones remain unable to shoot HQ images of subject matter close up and personal, so our reward Instagram photography suggestion is that you would have to get your hands on the macro zoom lens, like the *TrueLux macro zoom lens*.

What this zoom lens can do is allow your camera to target incredibly near to whatever you're shooting and then add visual interest (and depth) to your photograph, simultaneously.

5. <u>Don't Be Scared of the Silhouette</u>

That one seems just like a no-brainer, but many individuals continue to be afraid to embrace silhouettes on the Instagram grid.

First of all, ***what is a silhouette?*** *It's mostly when an object's form is captured against a gleaming light. It's not the same thing as a shadow.*

Silhouettes add an air of secret to an image, and against an extremely bright background, a silhouette really can look quite beautiful on your Instagram feed!

Another best part concerning this particular Instagram photography technique is that it is really simple to create images of a silhouette on your iPhone. You just need to know what you want to take a picture of, and then capture towards the light. That's it!

If you'd like to ensure that your subject's silhouette looks unmistakable but still dark, check out your iPhone camera app, tap the screen to create the focus, and then swipe right down to darken the camera exposure - you can still darken the subject even further with photography editing apps.

The optimum time to consider silhouette photographs, despite having your iPhone, is during what professional photographers refer to as the *golden hours of sunrise and sunset*. When sunlight is low coming, then you can position the source of light behind the topic, which means that you'll get a perfectly coloured sky as the background - taking benefit of tips 1 to 4.

You do not necessarily have to hold back for the golden hour to consider silhouette photographs, so long as your source of light is behind the subject.

For instance, if you are shooting indoors, you merely have to put your subject before the window (to consider advantage of daylight), or before a band light/ softbox if daylight is no option.

CHAPTER 10

Secret iPhone Camera Features Strange to You

Do you want to make the full use of your iPhone 11 Series (iPhone 11, iPhone 11 Pro, and iPhone 11 Pro Max) camera when you take photographs? As it's easy to take a photo with your iPhone, the excellent and crucial iPhone digital camera features are hidden from regular iPhone users. So, in this section, you'll find out the concealed iPhone camera features that every iPhone users must use.

- Swipe Left for Swift Access to Your iPhone Camera. How often have you seen or witness an incredible scene in front of your eyes, only to discover that it's gone at the time you're prepared to take a photo? You can improve your possibilities of taking a perfect shot if you know how to use your camera effectively.

- In case your iPhone is locked, you can press the home button to wake up your phone, and then swipe left through the lock display.

- The camera would open immediately, and you won't even need to enter your password to unlock your iPhone 11 Series (iPhone 11, iPhone 11 Pro, and iPhone 11 Pro Max). This trick would make you begin capturing in less than a second!

- However, what if you're already making use of the iPhone, and also you want to access the digital camera quickly, swipe up from the lower part of the screen to open the Control Centre as shown below.

From here, select the camera icon in the bottom right, and you're ready to start taking pictures!

How to Set Focus and Exposure

If you haven't set focus and exposure, the iPhone 11 Series (iPhone 11, iPhone 11 Pro and iPhone 11 Pro Max) can do it for you automatically. Usually, it can be a reasonably good job. Furthermore, that's how most iPhone users take almost all their photographs.

There are a few times, though, when autofocus fails - or when you wish to Focus on something in addition to the apparent subject.

That's when you'll want to create focus manually. That is super easy to do - Tap the location on the display where you'd prefer to set Focus, and the camera deals with others.

What distinction does the *focus* make? If you go through the picture above, the Focus is defined on the blossom in the foreground. The topic is bright and shiny, as the bloom petals and leaves in the background are blurred.

When you Tap on the screen to set Focus, the camera automatically sets the exposure. The exposure refers to improving the brightness of an image. So it's essential to get the exposure right if you are taking your picture.

*NB: When you wish to set **Focus**, check out the display to find out if the lighting of the image appears suitable. If* *it seems too vibrant or too darkish, you can change exposure before taking the picture.*

After you've Tapped on the screen to create focus and exposure, the exposure slider with a sun icon would be observed. Swipe up to help make the picture brighter or right down to make the image darker.

Efficaciously setting focus and exposure is one of the primary element skills that a photographer must master. When it takes merely a few Taps to modify focus and exposure, you must do it effectively to Focus on the most crucial components of the complete picture.

The task is that every photograph takes a specific method of focus and exposure setting.

Things that work notably for landscapes don't work almost as properly for night or tour photos.

How to Lock Focus and Exposure with AE/AF Lock

The iPhone also allows you to lock each one of the appealing points; focus and exposure. So why would you need to close those functions while going for a picture?

- The principle motive is if anything changes in the scene, including a moving subject or altered lighting, your focus and exposure would stay unchanged.

- That's why it's a great idea to lock Focus and exposure when you're expecting motion within the picture. For instance, *Focus and exposure* lock could be beneficial in street picture taking.

- You might frame the shot, and set the focus and exposure earlier, then obviously watch out for a person to pass-by before taking your photo.

- Once you've locked the focus and exposure, you might take several pictures of the same image and never have to set focus and exposure each time you want to consider photos. To unlock Focus and exposure, select anywhere on the screen.

- To lock focus and exposure, Tap and retain your hands on the display screen for mere multiple seconds at the stage where you want to create the centre point. A yellowish package with AE/AF lock can look near the top of the display.

***Note:** You can nevertheless swipe up or down on display to regulate exposure manually.*

*Now regardless of what happens within the framework or how you fling the iPhone 11, iPhone 11 Pro, and iPhone 11 Pro Max, the **Focus and Exposure** would still be unchanged.*

How to Take HDR Photos

HDR, which means *High Active Range*, is another incredible picture tool that is included in the camera of your iPhone 11, iPhone 11 Pro, and iPhone 11 Pro Max.

HDR picture taking with the iPhone combines three unique exposures of precisely the same image to produce one nicely exposed picture.

It's exquisite for high comparison moments with shiny and darkish areas since it allows you to capture extra components in both shadows and the highlights fully.

Some small adjustments within an editing application such as Snapseed can indeed draw out the colours and detail that were captured in the **HDR photograph**, although it still comes with fantastic well-balanced exposure.

- You'll find the HDR setting on the left side of the camera app. Tapping on HDR provides you with three options: Motion, ON, or OFF.

- Notably, it's high-quality to use HDR for panorama or landscape pictures and scenes where the sky occupies a significant area of the photograph. This enables the taking of extra fine detail in both the brighter sky and the darker foreground.

- There are a few downsides to HDR, especially in conditions of pictures of motion. Because HDR is a variety of three sequentially captured photos, you might encounter "ghosts" if the picture is changing quickly. HDR images also require a long period to capture, which means that your hands may shake even while the shutter is open up.

- It's additionally essential to state that non-HDR pictures will sometimes look much better than HDR ones, that's the reason it's a good idea to save lots of each variation of the image. To make sure that each variant is stored, go to configurations >

photos & camera, and ensure Save Normal Picture is **ON** in the *HDR section*.

- It's also well worth mentioning that the default iPhone 11 Series (iPhone 11, iPhone 11 Pro and iPhone 11 Pro Max) camera application comes with an alternatively subtle ***HDR impact,*** a sophisticated camera application that can create much more powerful HDR results and provide you with complete control over the catch.

How to Take Snapshot in Burst Mode

- Burst mode is one of the very most useful capturing features in the iPhone 11 Series (iPhone 11, iPhone 11 Pro and iPhone 11 Pro Max)'s camera app. It enables you to take ten images in only one second, which makes it easy to capture the suitable movement shot with reduced blur entirely.

- If you wish to activate a *burst setting*, press down the shutter button for half a second or longer, and the iPhone begins capturing one after another. When you've shot a burst of snap photos, after that, you can choose the lovely images from the Set and delete others.

- Burst setting is worth using each time there's any movement or unpredictability in the picture.

Remember utilizing it when photographing kids, animals, birds, and splashing water.

It's also excellent for taking pictures on magical occasions in street picture taking. Likewise, try the utilization of burst setting to capture the correct stride or present.

How to Take Pictures with Volume Buttons

Perhaps you have ever overlooked or missed the iPhone's tiny on-display shutter button? If so, change to the utilization of volume control keys beside your iPhone 11, iPhone 11 Pro, and iPhone 11 Pro Max!

Either of these buttons can be utilized for shutter release, and the tactile opinions you get from pressing this button is a great deal more pleasurable than pressing an electronic switch.

Additionally, this enables you to carry the iPhone with two hands, just as you'd grab a typical digital camera.

The only drawback of the approach is that you'll require pressing the Volume button pretty hard, which might produce camera shake. That's especially essential in a low-mild or less lighted environment, where any movement of your iPhone 11 Series (iPhone 11, iPhone 11 Pro and iPhone 11 Pro Max) would lead to the blurry picture.

How to take Photographs with your Apple Headphones

Remember those white apple headphones that were included with your iPhone 11, iPhone 11 Pro, and iPhone 11 Pro Max, on purchase can be utilized for photo taking. It additionally has *Volume buttons*, and you may use these control keys to consider photos!

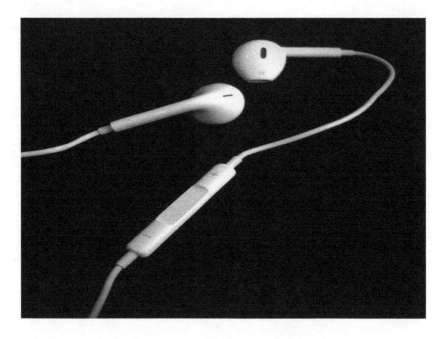

This feature is tremendously useful when you need to take discreet pictures of people you don't recognize or know in person, as you could pretend to be paying focused attention to music or making a call while you're taking pictures.

This method additionally is available when your iPhone 11 Series (iPhone 11, iPhone 11 Pro and iPhone 11 Pro Max) is on a tripod. As you release the shutter with your headphones, you can get rid of any unintentional digital camera movement, which is quite essential for night time pictures, long exposure images, etc.

CHAPTER 11

How to Use iPhone Portrait Mode to Make Blurry Background

The **iPhone 11 Series (iPhone 11, iPhone 11 Pro and iPhone 11 Pro Max) portrait mode** is the correct device to make brilliant looking portrait photographs with your iPhone 11 Series (iPhone 11, iPhone 11 Pro and iPhone 11 Pro Max). The portrait setting allows you to produce a shallow depth of field in your pictures quickly. This leads to an excellent blurry background that could typically be performed with a **DSLR camera**. With this section, you'll see how to use the iPhone 11 Series (iPhone 11, iPhone 11 Pro and iPhone 11 Pro Max) portrait setting to make a professional-looking iPhone 11 Series (iPhone 11, iPhone 11 Pro and iPhone 11 Pro Max) photo with a beautiful background blur.

What's Portrait Mode?

Portrait mode is a distinctive capturing mode available in the native camera application of an iPhone 11 Series (iPhone 11, iPhone 11 Pro and iPhone 11 Pro Max). It creates the use of a unique **Depth Impact Tool** to make a shallow Depth of field in your pictures.

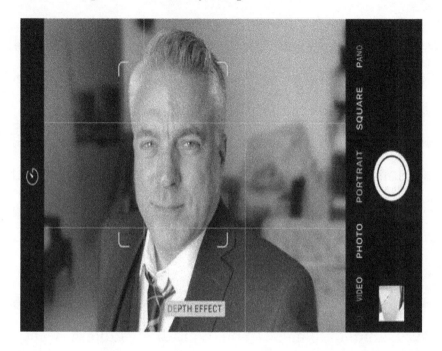

Shallow depth of field means that only a little area of the photo is within focus as the other is blurred. More often than not, you'll need your most significant concern at the mercy of appearing in razor-sharp focus as the background shows up blurred.

This soft and tender blurry background is categorized as "**bokeh**," which originates from the Japanese language.

Why Should You Use Shallow Depth of Field?

Portrait photographers often utilize the **shallow depth of field**. Why? Since it places the focus on the average person and creates a sensitive, dreamy background in it. Blurring the context is also truly useful when taking in locations with a busy, messy, or distracting background. The blurring makes the context secondary, getting the viewer's attention back to the main subject matter in the foreground.

Shallow Depth of Field isn't something you'd use for every kind of picture. You typically wouldn't want a blurry Background in scenery or architectural photo as you'd want to see everything vividly from foreground to Background.

However, in portrait pictures, a Shallow Depth of Field can make a significant distinction to the result of your photo. By blurring the background, you may make your subject matter stand out.

How to Develop Background Blur Using an iPhone 11 Series (iPhone 11, iPhone 11 Pro and iPhone 11 Pro Max)

Sometimes back, the iPhone 11 Series (iPhone 11, iPhone 11 Pro and iPhone 11 Pro Max) camera hasn't allowed you to have any control over the depth of field for your pictures. You've had the choice to have everything in Focus - unless your most significant subject matter comes very near the zoom lens, in such case, the background seems blurred.

However, with portrait setting on the new iPhone 11 Series (iPhone 11, iPhone 11 Pro and iPhone 11 Pro Max), now you can pick and choose what's in focus and what isn't. This gives you unprecedented control over your iPhone 11 Series (iPhone 11, iPhone 11 Pro and iPhone 11 Pro Max) camera, permitting you to mimic the appearance of DSLR cameras that can catch a shallow depth of field.

While portrait mode is most beneficial when planning on taking pictures of humans, pets, nature, etc., it can be utilized to blur the background behind any subject.

Many things appear better when there's a soft, dreamy background in it - especially if that background could distract the viewer from the primary subject.

How to use iPhone Portrait Mode

- Developing a shallow **Depth of Field** with Portrait mode on the iPhone is super easy. You can start by starting the default camera app, then swipe through the taking pictures modes (video, picture, etc.) until Portrait is highlighted in yellow.

- The very first thing you'll notice when you switch to Portrait Setting is that everything gets enlarged. That's because the camera automatically switches to the iPhone's 2x Telephoto Zoom lens. The telephoto zoom lens typically creates more flattering portrait images than the huge-angle zoom lens that could distort cosmetic features.

- You'll additionally spot the words **Depth Impact** appears at the bottom of the screen. Moreover, your telephone will help you give on-screen instructions in case you don't have things framed up optimally for an enjoyable portrait shot. For instance, you'll possibly see Move Farther Away or even more Light Required:

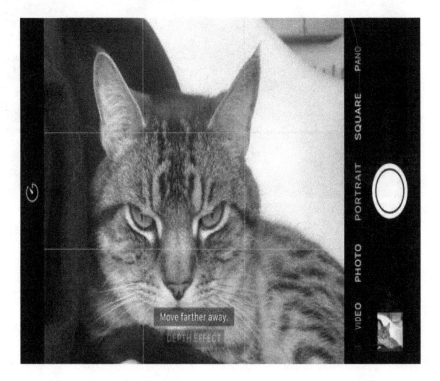

- The moment you're at the right distance from your subject, the words **Depth Effect** would be highlighted in yellow. You'll also see four yellow crop marks, indicating the face of your subject:

- You're now ready to take, so select the shutter button to consider your picture. After making the picture, you'll observe that two variations of the image can look in the camera app. One image will have the *Depth Impact* (blurred Background), and the other won't.

- Evaluating those two versions of the image sincerely suggests how nice a portrait picture shows up when it has a **Shallow Depth of Field**.

- If for reasons unknown you're not sure which of both pictures had the **Depth impact**, it'll be labelled in your image Set as shown below:

Tips For Creating Awesome Background Blur

When taking pictures with the iPhone portrait mode, it's essential to think about your background plus your subject. The type of Background you choose against its distance from your subject matter, will each have a significant effect on the final image.

The **Depth Effect** in Portrait mode is most effective when your subject matter is not the background. The further away the topic is from the background, the more delightful blur you'll get. Spot the difference in the background blur of the two pictures:

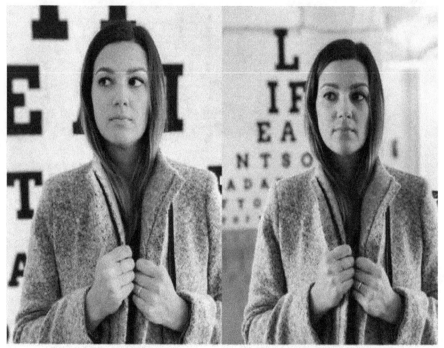

Subject close to background   Subject farther away from background

So; if your Background doesn't show up blurry enough when taking photos in a portrait setting, move your subject matter further from the background.

It's additionally essential to have something in the background so that there are a few components for the camera to blur.

Conclusively; the iPhone 11 Series (iPhone 11, iPhone 11 Pro and iPhone 11 Pro Max) has continuously been a first-rate device for most types of picture taking - such as landscape, structures, and street picture taking. However, now the iPhone 11 Series (iPhone 11, iPhone 11 Pro and iPhone 11 Pro Max) provides the potential to take amazing, high-quality portrait photos.

The telephoto zoom lens on the iPhone 11 Series (iPhone 11, iPhone 11 Pro and iPhone 11 Pro Max) is more flattering for shooting people than the typical wide-angle zoom lens.

As well as the **Magical Depth Impact tool** in the iPhone 11 Series (iPhone 11, iPhone 11 Pro and iPhone 11 Pro Max) Portrait Mode creates a lovely background blur - simulating the shallow depth of field that could formerly only be performed with a DSLR camera.

Taking photos with the iPhone 11 Series, (iPhone 11, iPhone 11 Pro and iPhone 11 Pro Max) portrait mode is a delight. Moreover, your subject will be thrilled when you suggest to them how beautiful they show up in your photos.

Don't forget; even while Portrait mode is the perfect setting when planning on taking pictures of individuals, pets, nature, etc., you can use it on any subject matter in which you require to make an attractive ***background blur***.

CHAPTER 12

How to Shoot Unique iPhone Photos

Hipstamatic is an elegant iPhone camera application for growing unique photos with a retro or vintage appearance. It comes with an outstanding selection of analogue film, zoom lens, and flash results, which enable you to easily change an ordinary picture into something exceedingly thrilling, stunning or dramatic. Besides, it comes with an accessible improving and editing Set for fine-tuning your photographs in post-processing. With this section, you'll learn the step-by-step instructions when planning on taking pictures and editing and enhancing lovely images using the Hipstamatic app.

Hipstamatic Zoom Lens & Film Combos

Hipstamatic is most beneficially known because of its potential to make a vast selection of retro-styled pictures based on numerous filters. The filter systems are applied when you take the photo; nevertheless, you can always change the ultimate result by just selecting different filter systems once you've used the shot.

The Hipstamatic filters get into three categories that are: zoom lens type, film type, and flash type. Before you proceed with going for a picture in Hipstamatic, you should select which zoom lens, film, and flash you want to use.

The lens decides the colours and tones in your photo. The film determines the framework or vignette across the advantage of the image (and occasionally also changes the colours of the image). The flash helps in creating distinctive lights.

The lens, film, and flash mixtures in Hipstamatic are known as *"combos."* Through the utilization of diverse combinations of the zoom lens, film, and flash, you can create an enormous variety of image styles - from faded superior results to high comparison dark and white pictures.

To give an example of how Hipstamatic can change an ordinary picture into something a lot more aesthetically attractive, check the photographs below. The first picture is the original photo without Hipstamatic filter systems applied:

Subsequent are a few examples of the same scene captured with the use of specific Hipstamatic lens and film combos:

When taking a picture with Hipstamatic, you can either permit the app to select a combo for you or try different mixtures of your desire until you locate an impact you like.

Hipstamatic includes a core set of lenses, film and flash options, and many more can be found as in-app purchases.

Selecting A Camera Interface

Hipstamatic has two different camera settings/interfaces included in the application. You may use the vintage camera user interface that mimics the appearance and feel of old film cameras:

You can likewise Utilize the *Pro camera interface,* which has a modern and professional feel. This camera mode is excellent if you want a bit of manual control while taking pictures:

If you wish to select from both camera settings, Tap both opposing arrows icon (arrows are either facing each other or aside depending on which digital camera setting you are employing).

How to Take Pictures with Hipstamatic Vintage Camera

You are going to learn how to consider pictures using the vintage camera mode in Hipstamatic. Be sure you've chosen the primary camera interface. If you're presently in the pro camera setting, select the opposing arrows to change to a traditional setting.

When working with Classic mode, you can change between your front and back views of the camera by Tapping the flip icon (curved arrow) in the bottom right of the screen.

How to Take a Picture with Basic Camera

- When you point the camera at a picture, you'll view it in the *sq. Viewfinder*. When capturing, you can choose from viewfinder alternatives.

- You can both view the picture with no filter

systems (lenses, movies, etc.) applied, alternatively, you can see in real-time, what the actual photograph can look like following when the shot has been taken using your chosen filters (you'll understand how to select lens, movies, etc. later as you read further).

- To change between those two viewfinder options, Tap the small dark switch in the bottom right of the viewfinder (as shown below):

When the switch is at the **OFF** function (completely black colour), you won't start to see the picture with all of your selected filters applied, but, when the photograph is used, the filters will be employed to the image when the switch is within the ON position (yellow eyeball icon will be shown).

I endorse getting the viewfinder change in the ON position, and that means you can easily see the impact of the existing zoom lens, film, and flash combo.

When you've composed your shot, take the picture by Tapping the yellow shutter button at the very top right.

NB: You can additionally enlarge the viewfinder by double-Tapping the viewfinder windows. You'll be able to select the viewer once to consider the shot.

If you wish to start to see the picture you've taken, Tap the square image thumbnail icon in the bottom still left of the screen. The image gallery can look displaying a preview of the photos you've shot with Hipstamatic, as shown below.

If you wish to see a much larger model of a specific photo, select the picture you want to see.

When viewing the entire sized image, you'll see which film/zoom lens/flash combo used, as well as the location where the picture was taken.

How to Decide on a Zoom lens/Film/Flash Combo

- For you to specify the appearance and design of your picture, you'll need to pick from the several options of lens and film (and flash if preferred).

- You can either decide on a preset combo from the favorites screen, or you create your combo from scrape. Taking into consideration the preset combo, first of all, begin by Tapping the circular icon (the next from the cheapest right-hand part) as shown in the red group below:

- Swipe across to see the number of cameras with diverse zoom lens/film/flash combos, however; don't Tap on the cameras yet. Every camera comes with an example photo showing the type of picture style that unique combo will generate.

- Tap and keep a camera to see more information in what configurations to be Utilized, then select the x to come back to the standard display screen.

- To select a specific combo from the favorites screen, Tap on the camera combo you want to use. On the other hand, you can allow the app to shuffle the combo on every occasion arbitrarily you are taking picture shot, providing you with a definite effect for every chance. If you like this option, select the shuffle icon (two arrows at the top right) and pick your chosen option:

- When you've selected a camera combo from the listed favorites, or the shuffle option, you'll be taken back to the camera to be able to begin capturing.

- You can additionally create your own lens/film/flash combos and upload these to the report on favorites. To achieve that, Tap the spherical icon (second from right hands side) at the bottom of the screen to access the preferences display.

- Swipe over the cameras to the much right, then select the newest favorites (+) icon.

- The proceeding screen will show a preview image with three icons beneath it. From still left to right, these icons are **Zoom lens, Film, Flash.**

- Begin by selecting the type of zoom lens that you want to use - recollect that the zoom lens adjusts the colors and shades of your picture when you choose the particular lens at the bottom of the screen, the preview image changes showing what impact that zoom lens could have on your photo.

- When you've chosen the lens that you like, Tap the Film icon (middle icon) under the picture preview. The film determines the framework or vignette round the advantage of the image, and additionally, it may change the firmness. Pick the film style that you want from underneath of the display:

- Next, select the flash icon (right-hand icon) under the image preview. The flashes put in a particular lightning impact on your picture. If you wish to apply flash, choose your decision from underneath of the display, typically, select No Flash.

- You'll discover that there's an advantage (+) indication for the zoom lens, film and flash options

- Tapping this icon goes to the Hipstamatic store where you can buy new lenses, movies, and flashes to increase your Sets.

- When you're pleased with your selected combo, Tap Save at the very top right part of the screen. On the next screen, you can enter a name for your combo, then select Done:

- Your newly added combo can look in the set of Favourites. To use this combo, select onto it, and also you'll be taken back to the camera and that means you can begin snapping:

- There's one other method of choosing a combo of a zoom lens, film and flash for capturing. Remember, there's a back view and front side view in traditional camera setting - on the back camera view, Tap the **Turn icon** (curved arrow in the bottom right) that may change you to the leading camera view.

- To select a particular zoom lens, swipe over the large zoom lens in the center of the display till you start to see the zoom lens you desire.

- To choose a film, select the film icon at the still left of the display screen. Swipe up or down on the rolls of the film until you find the lens you wish.

- To find out more records regarding a specific film, as well as test pictures, Tap the motion of the film - select Done to exit the film information.

- When you've selected the film you want to use, Tap the camera body at the right of the screen to return to the leading camera view.

- To select away a flash, select the **Flash icon** (second from lower still left) then swipe over the distinctive flash options. If you don't want to use flash, choose the No Flash option. Tap Done to come back to the leading camera view.

- If you wish to buy more lenses, movies, and

flashes to increase your Sets, Tap the **SHOPPING CART SOFTWARE** icon (second from bottom level right). You will see the presented products or click on a particular item if you wish to exit the shopping cart software, Tap **Done**.

- When you're content with the zoom lens/film/flash combo which you've selected, select the **Flip icon** (curved arrow in the bottom right) to come back to the back camera view, then start taking pictures!

How to Switch Flash ON & OFF

When you're capturing with the back camera view, you'll observe a black colour slider below the sq. Viewfinder. This will help you to select if the flash should be brought ON or not if you are going for a picture.

Whenever the flash slider reaches the center, the flash is powered down.

When the flash slider is moved left, your selected flash effect will be applied to the photo; however, the flash at the front end of your iPhone X Series won't fire on.

When the flash slider is moved to the right, your selected flash effect will be employed to the photograph, and the flash at the front end of your iPhone X Series will fire to provide more light on your subject.

How to Change Shutter Speed

- At the very top right of the camera, the display is the **shutter speed dial**. Modifying the shutter rate does a couple of things - it changes the exposure of the image (how gleaming it seems) and impacts how motion is captured.

- The lower the Volume on the dial, the slower the shutter speed. A slow shutter acceleration results in a brighter image, and an effortless shutter swiftness leads into a darker picture. You might use this feature to produce artistically shiny photos or very darkish moody pictures.

- Inside a case where you're capturing a scene with moving subjects, a natural shutter rate will freeze movement, and a sluggish shutter rate will capture the action as a blur.

How to Create Multiple Exposures

Hipstamatic gives you to generate thrilling dual exposure pictures. You take two different pictures, and then your camera combines them. That is a fun strategy to apply and can result in some exciting artwork and abstract images.

- To begin with, creating this kind of photograph, slide the **Multiple Exposure switch** (at the top left-hand side of the camera display) left such that it turns yellowish:

- Take your first picture by Tapping the yellow shutter button at the right. You will notice that the multiple exposure switch has moved to the right such that only half of the yellow square is seen:

- Position your camera at a different subject matter or view, then take the next shot. You'll start to see the "**Multi Revealing**" message show up as the app combines both images.

- If you wish to view the two times exposure image on your gallery, select the square model thumbnail icon at the bottom left of the screen. Tap the yellow pub near the top of the gallery to come back to the camera.

- Given that you're familiar with the functions of the vintage camera user interface, let's consider the procedure of taking pictures with the *Pro camera mode*.

How to Take Pictures with Hipstamatic Pro Camera

Hipstamatic pro camera mode gives more advanced camera application that gives you more manual control when shooting pictures.

- If you're presently using the Vintage camera mode, change to the pro camera user interface by just Tapping both opposing arrows at the low area of the screen as shown below:

- The pro digital camera interface appears very distinctive to the classic interface which doesn't have any retro styling, but has a larger square viewfinder with icons around the edges:

- Let's begin the usage of those camera icons to customize the final picture. In case you're using the camera in landscape orientation, as shown above, the top-right icon allows you to change the **Aspect Ratio**:

- The Aspect ratio decides the width and height of images. Choosing the 1:1 aspect percentage will result in an excellent square image, as the 16:9 proportion will be full than its elevation. The next icon in the red circle below gives you to choose different flash options, including *Flash On, Flash Auto,* and *Constant Light*:

The icon under the flash icon will help you to switch to the front camera to be able to have a self-portrait. While in the bottom right of the display will be the two opposing arrows that may take you back to the **Classic vintage style** camera.

The icon in the bottom left of the screen gives you to choose which zoom lens/film/flash combo you should employ - similar from what you did with the entire classic camera mode:

After Tapping the icon, you can progressively swipe

through the various combos until you locate an effect that suits your interest, or Tap the plus (+) icon to create a new combo. Tap on the combo you want to apply to return to the camera:

The **"M"** icon (at the right-hand side of the shutter button as shown below) stands for **Manual**, and it permits you to fine-tune the camera settings before taking your shot:

When you Tap the **Manual (m)** icon, a bar of icons will appear in its place:

The **round target icon** allows you to adjust the focus manually. The **magnifying glass icon** helps you to zoom in. Each of these settings is modified by making use of the slider at the bottom of the display screen.

The **+/- icon** turns on the exposure slider which lets you alter the brightness up or down for brighter or darker photographs:

For the fun part! The **ISO** and **Shutter Speed** (running man icon) settings allow you to manage and control exposure and how motion appears in your photograph:

- If you wish to create motion blur when photographing an instant running subject matter, you'll need a *slow shutter speed* and a *minimal ISO* (a minimum ISO facilitates preventing the picture from being over-exposed).

- To begin with, select the **ISO icon**, and use the slider to lessen the ISO to the lowest selection of number feasible. Then Tap the Shutter Rate icon (operating man) and move the slider to reduce the shutter rate to ensure that the picture appears almost too bright.

- The reason behind this is that; the brighter the picture, the slower the shutter acceleration, which equals higher movement blur of moving topics.

- If you're capturing in fantastic daytime conditions, you will learn that your sluggish shutter images appear too vibrant. That is why it's typically more comfortable to take at dawn or nightfall, or on darkish overcast times, to fully capture excellent show shutter photos.

- The final camera function is White Balance (lamp icon) that allows you to change the shade temperature on the scale from blue to yellow:

- The white balance enables you to warm up or keep down the colors, either to get perfect color balance or for creative impact. You can pull the slider left to help make the colors warmer (i.e., more yellow), and move to the right to make sure they are more refreshing (i.e., extra blue):

This is undoubtedly a proper setting for indoor capturing situations where the scene is illuminated by using artificial light with a yellow coloration cast. You can merely pull the white balance slider till you're pleased with the color firmness shown in the viewfinder:

How to Edit Pictures in Hipstamatic

Hipstamatic isn't taken into account as a professionally graded picture editor. It merely has a significant number of user-friendly improving features that will help you get the images simply perfect, such as the potential to choose a different combo such as zoom lens, film, and flash you can use when planning on taking pictures.

- To access the modifying mode, whether or not you're using the vintage camera or the pro camera, select the sq. Image thumbnail, which ultimately shows the previous picture taken:

- In the image gallery, Tap the picture you need to edit, then Tap the edit icon (3 circles) at the lowest part of the display screen as shown below:

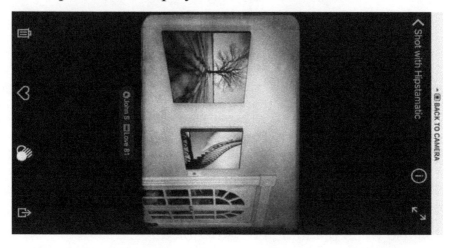

- Swipe through the preset combos at the bottom of the screen, Tapping on any that you prefer to see what impact it is wearing your image. Once you've chosen a preset that you want, use the slider to change the strength of the result till you're content with the final result. Tap **Save** when you're done editing.

- Much like the one-Tap presets, there are a few other modifying alternatives that you can use to improve your picture. Tap the edit icon (three circles), then select the choice icon (three sliders) situated merely above the configurations icon.

- Below your image, you'll visit a row of icons that may be used to fine-tune and edit the photo.

- Conclusively, Hipstamatic gives you to create an array of picture patterns, which include retro, classic, and dark and white.

- The application has two different kinds of camera settings (classic and pro), to be able to select to shoot using whichever interface you like. Each parameter can help you choose a zoom lens/film/flash combo, to enable you always to create the complete appearance and feel that you envisioned.

- The editing tools in the application enable you to fine-tune the picture when you've taken the shot, with the choice to decorate and improve the effect you used - or completely change the totality of the picture. With such a great deal of unique visual combos presented within this app, you can create excellent images, indeed with an incredible artistic edge.

CHAPTER 13
How to Use Superimpose Apps for Blending Images on iPhone

The superimpose application offers a fantastic group of gear for combining two iPhone photographs into a variety of approaches. You might change the background around your subject matter, put in a creative consistency overlay, or create a distinctive double exposure that mixes two photographs collectively. Superimpose additionally provides fundamental editing alternatives, including preset filters and color and exposure adjustments. With this section, you'll locate a way to use the superimpose application to replace the background in your iPhone photos and create an incredible double exposure impact.

How to Replace the Background of an Image

You can replace the background in virtually any iPhone picture with this process you are going to learn, which works satisfactorily with photos which have a smooth structure and a solid colour contrast between your subject and the background.

Follow the step-by-step instructions below meticulously.

Import Your Photos

When you open the superimpose app, you'll note there are four predominant areas as shown below that are *Home, Transform, Mask, and Filtering*. The application begins inside the home section, and that means you can import your pictures:

- When working on superimposes app, you will need to open both a background and a foreground picture. For the substance of changing background, the background image is the picture that will become the newest background. The foreground picture is the picture with most of your subject.

- To import your snap photos, ensure you're within the home portion of superimposing, then select the import icon (can be found at the top level of the screen). A section entitled import background can look close to the very best of the screen:

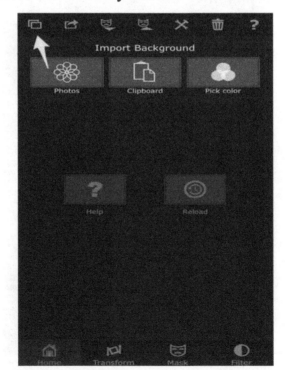

- In the import background section, Tap images to access your iPhone's picture library, then choose the photo you need to use as your background picture.

- When you insert or attach the background picture, you'll see its dimensions. If you wish to exchange the dimensional level, select Constraints for growth of varied size choice or crop the image as you want. In case your background-size doesn't require any modification, Tap **Choose**:

- Subsequently, you will have to import your foreground photograph. Tap the import icon again (it's located at the left of the display) and also you'll see a segment titled **import foreground** near the top of the display:

- Within the import foreground phase, Tap **Pictures**, then pick the image you wish to apply as your foreground photo.

Once more, you can crop the picture, resize it by using the **Constraints** choice, or Tap **Choose**:

Now, you'll see that your foreground picture is superimposed over the background image:

How to Reposition Foreground Image

Now you can resize and reposition the foreground image, and that means you can have it in the right position over the background image. For you to now access the resizing and repositioning tools, select the Transform option at the bottom of the screen.

You'll remember that the foreground picture will have deals on the edges (for resizing) and the sides (for rotating). If you wish to move the foreground image around, pull the image with your finger. The image may also be resized by pinching in and from the picture.

Near the top of the Transform display, you'll observe seven different icons. These are:

- **Undo**: This function is to undo your last action.
- **Redo:** This function is to redo your previous action.
- **Merge:** This function is to merge the background and foreground photos collectively with the reason to weigh another foreground picture at the very top. That's useful if you want to add extra layers to your image.
- **Swap:** This functions carefully turn the foreground picture horizontally or vertically, besides, to change the background and foreground photos.
- **Place at the Middle:** This function will position the foreground image within the guts of the background photo.
- **Fit to Background:** This function will level the foreground picture to the same size as the

background.

- **Configurations:** This function will change the transparency and blend setting, which would be needed for developing dual exposure images.

How to Produce Masks

The masking feature will enable you to edit and control the transparency of different sections of the foreground image(s).

When you make an integral part of the foreground picture transparent, the background image below will be seen. Quite merely, masking provides you with the liberty to remove undesirable servings of the foreground images.

You can perform this by Tapping the Mask option at the lowest area of the screen, then subsequently Tap the *Magic Wand icon* close to the right hand, which is below it to get access to the masking tools:

NB: There are six simple masking tools which are accessible (the top six tools are displayed in the pop-up menu, as shown below):

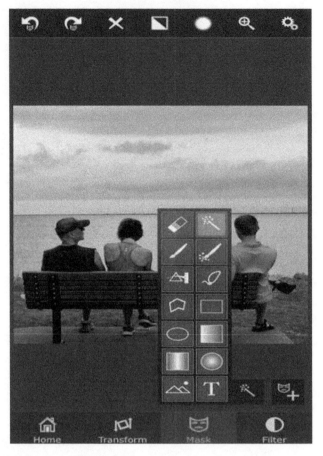

Below is a brief explanation of the six masking tools:

- **Eraser:** This tool will erase any errors you've manufactured in masking.

- **Magic Wand:** This function will mask all the similar coloration pixels encircling any point you Tap. You can drag or select to use the tool.

- **Brush:** Covers the whole area much, just like a brush. This tool doesn't recognize sides, so it's much useful for masking more significant regions.

- **Smart Brush:** This feature is comparable to the brush tool, but it recognizes the sides of the areas you're masking. Its function is to permit your selected exact locations and minimizes unintended or **unintentional brush strokes.**

- **Colour Range:** This function is similar to the magic wand tool, but instead of just the encompassing pixels, it selects all pixels related to the picture that fits the colour of the pixel you Tap.

- **Lasso:** This feature will help you to pull a freehand lasso and mask anything in or from the lasso loop.

NB: Every one of the tools has configurations ascribed to it. When you've chosen the masking tool, you want to use, Tap the configurations icon (can be found at the top right corner of the screen). The configurations for the tool can be seen close to underneath the screen, as shown below:

For example, you'll have the ability to regulate the ***Brush size, Strength and Smoothness, the Threshold, and Mask Advantage.*** **Threshold** determines the effectiveness of the Mask, and Mask Advantage will help you to choose a razor-sharp or smooth advantage.

If you wish to pick a part of the foreground image that you need to make transparent, select, or pull your finger over the regions you want to mask. A red dot will be shown to enable you to understand and start to see the real place where you're focusing on:

- You'll additionally observe a pop-up. You can pinch out to focus on; to be able to get a far more in-depth view of small areas and fill up the region with an increase of accuracy. You can likewise pinch directly into zoom back to view the complete image.

- If you wish to view the areas you've masked more clearly, select the view masks icon (second icon at the very top right corner):

You will find four view masks alternatives that show exceptional colored backgrounds, as shown below (checkerboard, red, green, or blue color). This depends on the colors on your foreground picture because some colored backgrounds will screen your selection flawlessly.

You can maintain focus on masking your film at the same time by using the colored masks views, or you might change to regular pictures where you can view the background image as you Tap the View Masks icon near the top of the display.

Save Your Valuable Masks

- After you've used the mask tools to ensure regions of your foreground image are apparent and transparent, departing merely the area of the image that you want to superimpose on the background, it's a perfect concept to store your masks in the Masks library.

- This is recommended because it will help you to apply that mask on some other focus on another photo. Moreover, if you're likely to superimpose the area of the foreground picture onto every other historical photo, you'll only be asked to mask the foreground photo once.
- You might then import it onto any background picture every time you want to utilize it, which can save you from needing to mask the parts of this image every time.
- This **Mask Library** is obtainable in the home segment of the app, Tap the home option at the low area of the screen. You can select the Save Mask icon (the middle icon at the top of the screen) to save lots of the **Mask** and then Tap **Save.**

Whenever you're set to apply that masks again to a different background photo, Tap the **Load Mask** icon (third icon from the top left) in the **Home** section of the app:

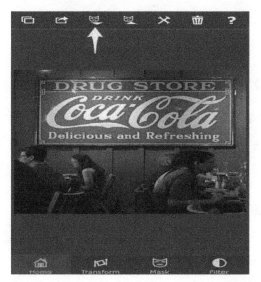

You'll now see the entire masks which you saved.

You can then Tap the masks you want to apply to place it onto your background image:

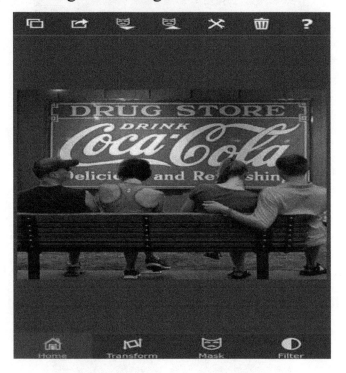

- **Save your Photo**

Whenever you're ready to save your final photograph, Tap the Export icon (second icon from the top left-hand side) in the Home section of the app. In the *Export Destination*, you can select photos to save the picture on your iPhone's photo library:

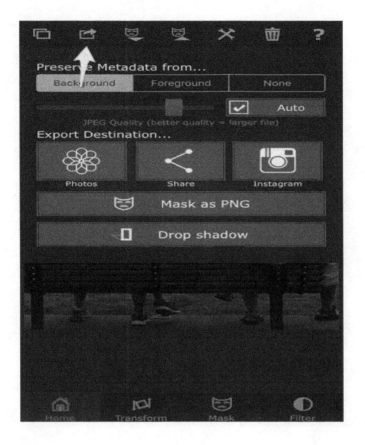

- **Delete the Session**

In case you choose to start the complete process again, Tap the Trash icon near the top of the display to delete the whole session to begin anew.

- **How to Produce a Double Exposure Picture**

Using the superimpose approach, you can also create an extraordinary increase in exposure impact. This calls that you should mix two pictures instead of masking one of these.

It's quite easy to develop great portraits with **double exposure silhouettes** just as the example below:

That is likewise an advantageous way for including a **texture overlay** to your image, which allows you to make a grunge look or textured painterly style. Below are the steps to check out to get this done;

Import Your Photographs

In the home portion of the superimpose app, use the import icon at the top right-hand side to import your background and foreground photographs precisely as you did with the first approach described above.

As both pictures are imported, the foreground picture can look similar to the background picture, as shown below:

How to Blend the Pictures

You can start by Tapping the **Transform option** at the low area of the screen. This section is not limited by enabling you to reposition and resize your foreground picture; nonetheless, it additionally gives you access to change the transparency and mix mode.

To demand **Mix mode**, select the Settings icon at the very top right part of the display:

- **Mix mode** provides unique techniques; both pictures can also built-in together through the modification of presented tools such as comparison and brightness.

- The **Mix mode** is defined to default typically. It is one option to keep carefully the blend mode arranged to Normal and use the opacity slider to change the transparency of the foreground picture.

- Another approach is to see different blends of both pictures using a few of the other blend mode options, which consist of Multiply, Screen, Overlay, etc.

- You can merely Tap on the few different combination modes to observe how they have an impact on your final picture. Placing under consideration, the example below, Overlay, Colour, and Difference, was used. Each one of these creates a unique and fantastic mixture of both pictures:

How to Change the Filter

- Tapping the Filter option in the bottom of the screen will enable you to apply a growth of preset filtration system results to beautify the image. There are also adjustments presented tools for *color hue, saturation, exposure, brightness, comparison, color balance, and blur.*

- You might use these results to each one of the foreground and background images. It's a step that isn't usually necessary, but it's a false choice to have.

- Near the top of the display, choose whether you want to focus on the foreground or background image. Just select the configurations icon at the very top right part of the screen, and also you'll visit a pass on of adjustment configurations you can use:

Moreover, within the Filter segment, Tap the **FX** icon to access 33 distinctive preset filters, as shown below:

You can effortlessly change the filter on either of the pictures or both, creating unlimited blend feasibilities. Below are some examples of double exposure image with distinctive filters implemented:

When you've completed the editing process of your photograph, you can return to the home section to save your picture.

Summarily, superimpose is a remarkable app for changing backgrounds of pictures, in addition to creating outstanding double exposure photos.

- All you have is a foreground image and a background image, and next use the superimpose software to masks and mix both pictures as you wish.

- Whenever you've actualized the *perfect blend*, don't neglect to check the filters and adjustment modifications to see when you can further improve your picture with distinct effects.

Once you have mastered the utilization of the superimpose app, after that, you can try advanced layer masking techniques. You can likewise make sure you browse the Leonardo App, which is a product of the same company. Leonardo helps several layers, a big group of image modifications, in addition to other editing and enhancing tools.

CHAPTER 14

The 4 Best Camera Application For iPhone

Looking for the best camera application for an iPhone Series? Even while the default iPhone Series camera application has some fantastic capabilities, sometimes you'll want a more sophisticated camera. However, with so many camera applications available online, it might be tough to discover which to use. This assessment of the five best iPhone Series camera applications will help you to find the right app for you.

VSCO: How to Use VSCO

You might already be familiar with the VSCO application as it's more popular because of its picture improving functions and beautiful movie-like filters. However, this free application also has an effectively integrated camera with many guide settings.

- If you are capturing in VSCO, you could have manual control of *Focus, Exposure, White*

Stability, as well as *ISO and Shutter Speed.* Depending on how new your iPhone, you may even have the ability to shoot in *Natural Mode.*

- To gain access to the camera in VSCO, open up the application, and swipe down with your finger. Once you are in the camera setting, you'll see numerous icons underneath (or the medial side, if you're making use of your phone horizontally) which may enable you to customize the camera configurations.

However, the above are just a few of the customizable options. If you swipe on the icons with your finger, you'll see there are very few extra "hiding" solely off display.

A significant number of the advanced camera features toggle among distinctive alternatives (flash, the grid, raw, and the funny "face overlay" choice), while some think of a slider for excellent fine-tuning settings with *exposure, white balance, focus, iso, and shutter rate.* For example, if you select on the solar icon, the exposure slider will be observed at the lower part of the display screen, as shown below.

- Pull the slider to change the exposure (brightness) of your picture. In case you want to return to the default automated exposure, select on the "A."
- The **White Balance (WB)** setting is utilized for

actualizing the right colors on your pictures by either starting to warm up or trying to cool off the colors. Use the slider to change the color heat in your image.

- You can view below two variations of the same image - one with a more relaxed white balance setting (bluer) and one with a warmer white balance setting (more orange). The color temp will have a significant effect on the overall temper of your picture.

The ISO setting controls the digital camera's sensitivity to light, and for that reason affects the exposure (brightness) of the photograph. The better the ISO Volume, the brighter the exposure maybe. However, retain in mind that high ISO configurations can result in grainy images.

Shutter Speed settings the exposure time for the picture. Lengthy exposures are perfect for night picture taking, blurring movement, and taking light trails.

When capturing lengthy exposure images, be sure you hold the camera still actually to avoid any camera tremble that brings about blurry pictures. Make use of a tripod for the product quality results.

While you're dealing with those types of manual settings in VSCO, you're essentially making the utilization of your iPhone as if you would use a manual DSLR camera.

VSCO can be an excellent application to use if you're merely starting or a dummy by using third-party camera apps. It's available for download from the application store and has a great selection of manual handles that will put in a level of course and creativeness to your pictures.

MANUAL: How to Use Manual

- If manual camera settings are what you're after, the aptly named manual application ($3.99) is just about the best replacement camera application for your iPhone. Quickly, you can transform the Shutter Speed, ISO, and exposure values to attain the creative impact you need.

- Unlike VSCO, you have the decision to manually control the camera settings, which include **Focus, White Balance, ISO, Shutter Speed,** and **Brightness (*called EV*).**

- The interface is quite intuitive. When you release the app, all the configurations are in automated mode. If you wish to change to manual control, select and hold on to the ISO or Shutter Speed, and you'll be able to access your configurations. Moreover, if you would like to restore to the automated setting, Tap the "A."

- You can even decide if you would like to snap images in Raw Layout, JPEG Layout, or both. Natural capture enables you to store images without compression, ensuring an excellent picture that provides you with more significant potential for improvement during editing. However, retain in mind that Natural photos take up plenty of more space for storage on your phone.

- There's a specific setting that may be great, which is the slow shutter speed.

- Another superb feature of the manual application is that you can by hand Focus on your subject. Just slip your finger left or directly on the Focus bar at the lowest area of the screen till your subject matter sometimes appears in perfect Focus. If you wish to go back to the auto-focus setting, select the AF button.

This app also offers a particular focusing device, rendering it more straightforward to focus manually. Once you start sliding the Focus bar, a middle square magnifies the subject, and that means you can test your important Focus thoroughly. This standard concentrating feature is particularly useful while taking up close or macro issues.

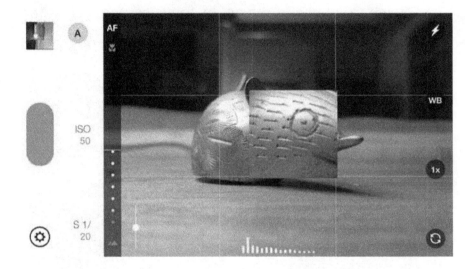

Having the ability to control those advanced manual settings provides you with more excellent alternatives as an iPhone X Series photographer, letting you create the best available picture, even in complex taking conditions.

CAMERA+: How to Use Camera+

Camera+ is a superb camera and picture enhancing app combined. It is the first advanced camera app I've seen great photographers using on iPhone, and you may set the middle point, and exposure one following the other, as the timer for the camera, could be arranged for 30 mere seconds.

- The camera+ programmer has continued to enhance the app over time, and it's now stronger than ever. All the classic features are just like they were; nevertheless, you could now use digital camera+ much as if you use the manual app. You can even shoot in Natural mode and extra control of your last photograph.

- In camera+ it's the simplest. It is easy to switch the center point, exposure, and white balance to creatively impact the feeling of your snap photos.

- To create the Focus and exposure individually, select on display with two fingertips at the same instant of your time. You'll visit an individual exposure factor (orange group) and Focus (red square). Pull the Focus and contact with distinctive elements of the picture until it appears the just as what you would like it to appear to be.

- If you wish to alter the shutter speed and ISO configurations, Tap the group icon above the shutter release button. A -panel will slip up, letting you by hand change the settings.

- The shutter speed setting appears on the left and the ISO at the right; swipe through each establishing to alternate them. To escape the manual configurations and came back to the default setting, you could either Tap the automated button or dual Tap the screen.

- Typically you will never need to disturb yourself about **white balance** because the iPhone does a notable activity of fabricating all the colorations to appear genuine. However, you can personally override the white balance placing to provide your photos with a different feel.

- You might use the shutter speed and ISO settings in camera+ to obtain computer images extraordinary impact evergreen exposures. In the example underneath, an image of a pool that experienced a lovely tree sculpture was captured.

The primary picture (above) converted into shot using the iPhone's default camera app. It made an appearance pretty good; nevertheless, the reflections and ripples in the water had been some distraction.

So let look at case research where the camera+ is utilized to shoot an extended exposure of the picture, as shown below. You will observe how the sluggish shutter speed has made water show up silky smooth. It makes the water significantly less distracting, and on the other hand, your vision is attracted to the tree.

Underneath you might observe how this impact in digital camera+. Indeed, when you have an iPhone, or later versions would be, digital camera+ will continue to work with either of the telephone's lens. Because of this shot, it was turned to the telephoto zoom lens (group icon near to top left) because the photographer couldn't get near to the tree without getting damp!

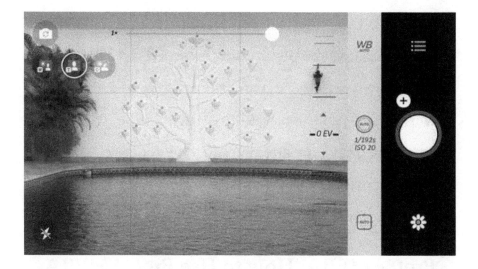

Moreover, subsequently, Tap the automatic button to show the manual controls. The shutter speed was set to an entirely long 8 seconds (with the iPhone set up on a tripod) and reduced the ISO value as little as reasonable (which on camera+ was 0.01) to make sure the photo didn't end up over-exposed (too brilliantly bright).

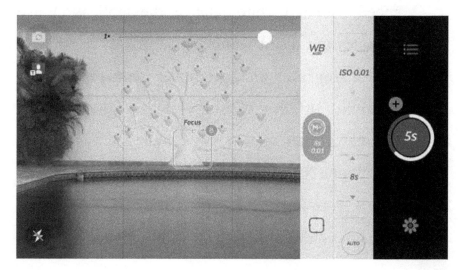

In the end, the spherical shutter button was tapped and watched because the picture was exposed over 8 seconds. Among many of these camera apps, camera+ is very powerful and can be a bit overwhelming. So I will recommend that you attempt out one function at a time and get accustomed to it before moving on to the next.

ProCAMERA: How to Use ProCAMERA

The ProCamera app, especially the latest version, gives you a remarkable number of control over your settings while taking pictures.

- Asides the usual manual controls like shutter speed, ISO and white balance, the application also includes advanced features like **RAW capture**, a **live histogram**, an **anti-shake feature**, and the capability to access either camera lens in the iPhone or later version of iPhone such as iPhone 11, iPhone XS, iPhone XR, etc.

- In case you're shooting in low light (or with the

telephoto zoom lens, when camera shake is more of a threat) and you don't have a tripod, attempt shooting with the use of the anti-shake mode.

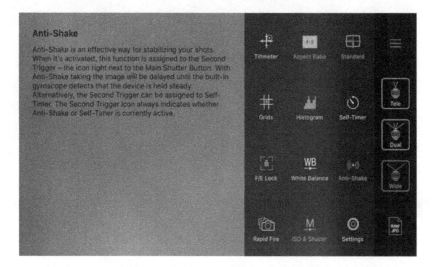

- This mode uses your iPhone's integrated intervalometer to gauge how much the telephone is moving. After that, it waits till you're securing to the camera at a sharp point before it requires a photo. That is a significant-excellent characteristic!

Once you want to modify shutter speed and ISO, you have options. The first option is by using a fully manual setting where you control both *ISO and Shutter Speed.*

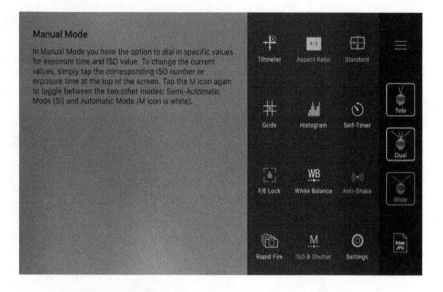

Manual Mode

In Manual Mode you have the option to dial in specific values for exposure time and ISO value. To change the current values, simply tap the corresponding ISO number or exposure time at the top of the screen. Tap the M icon again to toggle between the two other modes: Semi-Automatic Mode (SI) and Automatic Mode (M icon is white).

- The task with manual mode is you need to balance the shutter speed, and ISO settings are to be sure you get the exposure accurate (not too darkish not too shiny). In the event you're not used to the use of the settings, you will get this complicated to get right.

- Therefore, the second choice is to make by using **SI mode**, which enables you to change either the Shutter Speed or the ISO, and the application adjusts the option establishing to calculate the perfect exposure. This setting is exceptional if you're not used to the utilization of manual exposure settings.

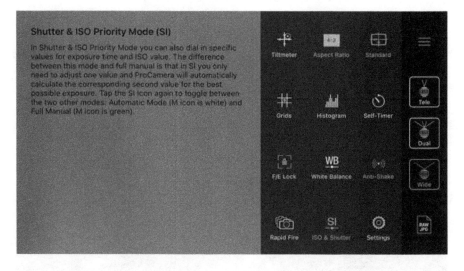

ProCamera additionally can customize the self-timer for any amount of time as much as 30 seconds, which is very beneficial.

For this image, the iPhone was set on a tripod, then set the timer delay to 20 seconds to provide sufficient time to walk into the shot for the photographer to be seen in the photograph.

- Another great function of the self-timer would be that the flash blinks each second until it requires the picture. It implies you don't need to be surprised at how time has exceeded and set up image has been used. After the blinking halts, you'll know you can get back to the iPhone to have a look at your shot indeed.

Finally, there are a variety of in-app purchases you may make if you want to try their HDR or low-light cameras. You can get from them a free trial to see what they do; however, you'll get a watermark on your picture until you purchase the application, which can make an optional setting available.

Chapter 15

Top iPhone 11 Tips & Tricks

Control Your Apple TV With iPhone 11

The Control Focus on the iPhone 11 has an impressive trick: it enables you to regulate your Apple TV if you have one. As long as your iPhone 11 and Apple Television are on a single cellular network, it'll work. Get into Control Centre and then look for the Apple Television button that shows up. Touch it and start managing your Apple Television.

How to Enable USB Restricted Setting on iPhone 11

Apple just built a robust new security feature into the iPhone 11 with the latest version of iOS; this launch is what's known as ***USB Restricted Setting*** to the iPhone 11. Lately, companies have been making devices that may be connected to an iPhone's USB slot and crack an iPhone's passcode.

To protect from this, Apple has introduced a USB Restricted Setting. USB Restricted Setting disabled data writing between an iPhone and a USB device if the iPhone is not unlocked to get more than one hour; this effectively makes the iPhone breaking boxes ineffective as they may take hours or times to unlock a locked iPhone.

By default, *USB Restricted Mode* is enabled in iOS. But for those who want to disable it, or make sure it hasn't been disabled, go to the *Configurations app* and touch *Face ID & Passcode*. Enter your passcode and then swipe down until you visit a section entitled *"Allow Access When Locked."*

The final toggle in this section is a field that says *"USB Accessories."* The toggle next to them should be turned OFF (white); this implies *USB Restricted Setting* is allowed, and devices can't download or upload data from/to your iPhone if the iPhone is not unlocked to get more than one hour.

Use Two Pane Scenery View

This tip only pertains to the iPhone 11 Pro Max but is cool nonetheless. If you keep your XS device horizontally when using specific applications, you'll see lots of the built-in apps changes to a two-pane setting, including Email and Records. This setting is the main one you observe on an iPad where, for example, you can see a list of all of your records in the Records app while positively reading or editing a single note.

How to stop iPhone 11 Alarms with Your Face

An extremely cool feature of the iPhone 11 is Face ID. It gives you to unlock your phone just by taking a look at it. Face ID also has various other cool features-like that one. Whenever your iPhone 11 or XS security alarm goes off, you could silent it by just picking right up your iPhone and taking a look at it; this tells your iPhone you understand about the arm, and it'll quiet it.

Quickly Disable Face ID

Depending on your geographical area, the police might be able to legally demand you uncover your smartphone at that moment via its facial recognition features. For reasons unknown, facial biometrics aren't protected in the manner fingerprints, and passcodes are; in a few localities. That's why Apple has generated an attribute that lets you quickly disable Face ID in a pinch without going into your settings. Just press the side button five times, and Face ID will be disabled, and you'll need to enter your passcode instead to gain access to your phone.

How to slow the two times click necessary for Apple Pay

Given that the iPhone 11 jettisoned the Touch ID sensor, you confirm your *Apple Pay* obligations by using Face ID and twice pressing the medial side button. By default, you would need to dual press the medial side button pretty quickly-but it is possible to make things slow down.

To take action, go to *Settings* > *General* > *Availability*. Now scroll right down to Side Button. Privately Button screen, you can select between *default, gradual, or slowest*. Pick the speed that is most effective for you.

Chapter 16

How to Create & Use iPhone 11 Shortcuts

How to Put in a Virtual Home Button to the iPhone

In respect to get a virtual Home button configured, you first have to allow the home button itself. Here's how:

- Touch *Settings*.

- Touch *General*.

- Touch *Accessibility*.

- Touch *AssistiveTouch*.

- Move the *AssistiveTouch* slider to On/green. The digital Home button shows up on your screen.

- Position the button anywhere on your screen using drag and drop.

- Make the button pretty much transparent utilizing the Idle Opacity slider.

- Touch the button to see its default menu.

How to Customize the Virtual Home Button Menu

To change the number of shortcuts and the precise ones that exist in the default menu:

- Around the _Assistive Touch_ screen, tap Customize Top Level Menu.

- Change the number of icons shown in the very best Level Menu with the plus and minus control keys at the bottom of the screen. The minimum volume of options is 1; the utmost is 8. Each icon represents a different shortcut.

- To improve a shortcut, touch the icon you want to improve.

- Tap one of the available shortcuts from the list that appears.

- Touch Done to save the change. It replaces the shortcut you have chosen.

- If you decide you want to return to the default group of options, touch Reset.

How to Add Custom Activities to the Virtual Home Button

Now that you understand how to include the virtual Home button and configure the menu, it is time to get to the nice stuff: custom shortcuts. As being a physical Home button, the digital button can be configured to react differently based on how you touch it. Some tips about what you must do:

Within the *AssistiveTouch* screen, go directly to the Custom Actions section. For that section, touch the action that you would like to use to result in the new shortcut. Your alternatives are:

- **Single-Touch**: The original single click of the home button. In cases like this, it's an individual touch on the digital button.

- **Double-Touch**: Two quick touches on the button; if you choose this, you can also control the Timeout establishing (i.e., the time allowed between touches) if additional time goes by between touches, the iPhone goodies them as two solitary touches, not a double-touch.

- *Long Press*: Touch and contain the virtual Home button. If you choose this, you can also configure a Duration, which sets how long you will need to press the screen because of this feature to be triggered.

- *3D Touch*: The 3D Touch screen on modern iPhones lets the screen respond differently based on how hard you press it. Utilize this option to have the digital Home button react to hard presses.

Whichever action you touch, each screen presents several options for shortcuts that you can assign to the action. They are especially cool because they change actions that may normally require pressing multiple control keys into an individual touch.

Most shortcuts are self-explanatory, such as Siri, Screenshot, or Volume Up, but a few need description:

- *Convenience Shortcut*: This shortcut may be used to cause all types of convenience features, such as inverting colours for users with eyesight impairment, turning on VoiceOver, and zooming in on the screen.

- *Shaking*: Choose this, and the iPhone responds to a button touch as if an individual shook the telephone. Shake pays for undoing certain activities, particularly if physical issues prevent you from shaking the telephone.

- *Pinch*: Performs the same as a pinch gesture on the iPhone's screen, which pays for people who've impairments that produce pinching hard or impossible.

- *SOS*: This button allows the iPhone's Emergency SOS feature, which causes a loud sound to alert others that you might need help and a call to Emergency services.

- *Analytics*: This feature starts the gathering of Assistive Touch diagnostics.

Chapter 17

iPhone Home Button Fundamentals

Possibly the most significant change Apple introduced using it's groundbreaking iPhone 11 was removing the home button. Because of the iPhone's debut, the home button has been the only button on leading the phone. It had also been the most crucial button since it was used to come back to the home screen, to gain access to multitasking, to consider screenshots, plus much more.

You can still do all those things on the iPhone 11, but how you need to do them differs. Pressing a button has been changed by a couple of new gestures that result in those familiar functions. Continue reading to learn all the gestures that changed the home button on the iPhone 11.

How to Unlock the iPhone 11

Waking the iPhone 11 from sleep, also called unlocking the phone (never to be puzzled with unlocking it from a phone company), continues to be very easy. Just grab the phone and swipe up from underneath the screen.

What goes on next depends upon your security configurations. Unless you have a passcode, you'll go to the Home screen. If you do have a passcode, Face ID may recognize that person and take you to the home screen. Or, if you have a passcode but avoid Face ID, you would have to enter your code. Regardless of your configurations, unlocking requires a simple swipe.

How to Go back to the Home Screen on iPhone 11

Having a physical Home button, time for the home screen from any application just required pushing a button. Even without that button, though, time for the Home screen is relatively simple.

Just swipe up an extremely brief distance from underneath the screen. An extended swipe does another thing (check another item to get more on that), but an instant little flick would need you out of any application and back to the Home screen.

How to Open up the iPhone 11 Multitasking View

On previous iPhones, double-clicking the home button raised a multitasking view that enables you to see all open up apps, quickly change to new apps, and easily quit applications that are working.

That same view continues to be on the iPhone 11; nevertheless, you get access to it differently. Swipe up from underneath in regards to a third of just how up the screen. It is just a little hard initially because it's like the shorter swipe that goes to the home screen.

Switching Apps Without Starting Multitasking on iPhone 11

Here's an example in which eliminating the home button presents an entirely new feature; it doesn't can be found on other models. Rather than having to open up the multitasking view from the last item to improve apps, you can change to a new app with only a simple swipe.

At the bottom corners of the screen, about a level with the line at the bottom, swipe still left or right. Doing that would leap you into the next or earlier application from the multitasking view a considerably faster way to go.

Using Reachability on iPhone 11

With ever-bigger screens on iPhones, it could be hard to attain things that are not your thumb. The Reachability feature that was first launched on the iPhone 6 series solves that. An instant double-touch of the home button brings the very best of the screen down, so it is simpler to reach.

In the iPhone 11, Reachability continues to be a choice, though it's disabled by default (transform it on by going to *Settings -> General -> Accessibility -> Reachability*). Whether it's on, you can gain access to the feature by swiping down on the screen near the collection in the bottom. That may be just a little hard to understand, and that means you can also swipe along rapidly from the same location.

New Methods to Do Old Jobs: Siri, Apple Pay, and More

You will find loads of other standard iPhone features that use the home button. Here's how to execute some of the most typical ones on the iPhone 11:

- *Take Screenshots*: Click on the Side and volume up buttons at the same time.

- *Change Off/Restart*: Press and contain the Part and volume up buttons at the same time.

- *Activate Siri*: Press and hold the Side button.

- *Confirm Apple Pay and iTunes/App Store Buys*: Use Face ID.

Where is the Control Centre?

If you know your iPhone, you might be wondering about the Control Centre. This useful group of tools and shortcuts is utilized by swiping up from underneath the screen on other models. Since swiping around underneath of the screen does so a great many other things on the iPhone 11, Control Centre is elsewhere upon this model.

To gain access to it, swipe down from the very best right part of the screen (to the right of the notch), and Control Centre appears. Touch or swipe the screen again to dismiss it if you are done.

Want a Home Button? Add One Using Software

Wish your iPhone 11 had a Home button? Well, you can't get a hardware button, but there's a way to get one using the software. The AssistiveTouch feature adds an on-screen Home button for individuals with physical conditions that prevent them from quickly clicking the home button (or for people that have broken Home buttons). Anyone can change it and use that same software/virtual button.

To allow AssistiveTouch:

- Touch *Settings*.

- Touch *General*.

- Touch *Accessibility*.

- Touch *AssistiveTouch*.

- Move the AssistiveTouch slider to On/green, and a button shows up on the screen that is capable of doing some of the home button's tasks.

Chapter 18

Using iPhone 11 without Home Button

Gestures on the iPhone's touchscreen will always be necessary, but without the Home button, the iPhone 11, and later models, gestures become essential. To execute functions just like a turnoff or time for the Home screen on your iPhone 11, 11 Pro and 11 Pro Max, you are going to use unique gestures that combine the medial side and Volume control keys instead of the lacking Home button.

Common features, like speaking with Siri, starting **Apple**

Pay, and shutting apps, will have unique gestures that Utilize your phone's physical control keys, Face ID, and the touchscreen. This chapter addresses all the tips you should know, like how to use Reachability, have a screenshot, as well as how to briefly disable Face ID the iPhone 11, 11 Pro and 11 Pro Max. Let's get started doing how to use gestures to get around iPhone models X and later.

There are a significant number of new gestures and changes to navigate the iPhone, given that Apple did away with the Home button. You're probably acquainted with the most common iPhone gestures, such as pinching with two fingertips to focus or Tremble to Undo. You can also pull multiple photos and drop them into another app. Gestures on the iPhone would always be an integral part of the routine. However, the iPhone 11 launched a lot of new ways to do old stuff. Unless in any other case, indicated these procedures all connect with the iPhone 11, 11 Pro, and 11 Pro Max.

How to Unlock Your iPhone with Raise to

Wake

Raise to Wake is fired up by default on the iPhone 11 and other newer models. To use *Raise to Wake* on the iPhone 11, 11 Pro and 11 Pro Max, lift your iPhone, and the screen would automatically start. If *Raise to Wake* isn't working, likely, you have accidentally handicapped the feature inside Configurations.

How to Enable Raise to Wake:

- Open up the *Settings* app.

- Select *Screen & Brightness.*

- Toggle Raise to Wake to the ON position to allow the feature.

You don't need to lift your phone awaken the screen on iPhone 11; you can merely touch the screen to awaken your iPhone 11, even if Raise to Wake is impaired.

How to Unlock the iPhone 11 & Newer iPhones

To unlock your iPhone 11, 11 Pro and 11 Pro Max, or 11, you would need to ensure that a Face ID is established. Using Face ID, you can boost or tap your iPhone 11, or other newer models, to wake and unlock your iPhone by looking straight at the screen.

How exactly to Unlock an iPhone 11 or Later Using Face ID:

- Wake the screen up by either tapping the screen or using Raise to Wake.

- Look directly at the screen to use Face ID to unlock your device.

- Swipe up from underneath of your Lock screen to visit the Home screen.

- If, for just about any reason, Face ID didn't unlock your mobile phone, swipe up from underneath of the screen to retry Face ID or even to enter your passcode instead. Once you have input your passcode, your iPhone will automatically go back to the Home screen, or whatever application was open up last.

How to Open up the Control & Notification Centres

The notch on the iPhone 11 and later models divide the very best of the screen into a left and right hands screen. On your own iPhone 11, 11 Pro and 11 Pro Max, the right part of the notch near the top of the screen is used to gain access to your Control Centre while the left side is utilized to open up Notifications.

- To open Control Centre, swipe down from the right-hand side of the screen.

- To open Notifications, swipe down from the left-hand side of the screen.

How to Go back to the Home screen From an App

Returning to the home screen can appear impossible if there is no Home button. Around the iPhone 11, 11 Pro and 11 Pro Max, and 11, you can go back to your home screen by following the instructions below.

How to Go back to the Home Screen:

- From within any app, place your finger on the home bar underneath the center of the screen.

- Swipe up toward the very top of your screen.

How to Activate Apple Pay

On previous iPhone models, twice tapping the home button raised Apple Pay from a locked screen, but on the iPhone 11 or later, you will have to use a new gesture to gain access to **Apple Pay**. To use Apple Pay from a locked screen on the iPhone 11, 11 Pro and 11 Pro Max, you will have to double click your side button and use Face ID to continue with Apple Pay. Here's how to use

Apple Pay on iPhones without a Home button:

- Double click on the Part button to open up Apple Pay

- Look into your iPhone screen to verify with Face ID.

If Apple Pay doesn't appear when the medial side button is double-clicked, 1 of 2 things is undoubtedly going on: either you haven't created a debit card with Apple Pay (check even though you have; my cards disappeared after establishing my new iPhone) or you do not have Apple Pay allowed in settings; this is fixed with the next steps:

- Open up the Settings app.

- Select Face ID & Passcode.

- Toggle ON **Apple Pay** under Use **Face ID** For.

How to Power Off the iPhone 11

Sometimes, you will need to power your iPhone off for a movie, a lecture, or other events that want your full attention. Like previous models, whenever your iPhone 11, 11 Pro and 11 Pro Max, are a runoff, then you will have to use a gesture to turn your iPhone back On carefully.

To carefully *Turn On* the iPhone 11 or later models, press and maintain the side button before the Apple logo design appears.

How to Access Siri with Side Button

Removing the home button also changes how you access Siri on the iPhone 11 and newer models.

- If you wish to use gestures rather than Hey Siri on the iPhone 11, 11 Pro and 11 Pro Max, then you will have to use the medial side button to gain access to Siri.

- Click and hold the Side button (formerly known as the Rest/Wake button) to speak to Siri.

How to Take Screenshots without the home Button

Sometimes, you would need to have a screenshot to save lots of a great formula as a graphic or to keep hold of a text to examine later.

- To have a screenshot on the iPhone 11, 11 Pro and 11 Pro Max, you'll use a mixture of the medial side and volume buttons rather than utilizing a Home button.

- To consider screenshot on your iPhone 11, or a later model iPhone, concurrently press and release the medial side button and Volume Up button.

How to Enable & Activate Reachability

Reachability slashes off the low fifty percent of the screen and moves the very best part of your screen to underneath, making it simpler to reach the very best of your display with one hand. By default, Reachability has switched off on the iPhone X, XS, XS Max, and iPhone 11 Series phone; nevertheless, you can allow the Reachability feature inside the Settings portion of your Configurations app.

To allow Reachability on your iPhone 11, 11 Pro, and 11 Pro Max:

- Open up the *Settings* app.

- Select *General.*

- Touch *Accessibility.*

- Toggle on *Reachability.*

- Swipe down on the home bar or bottom level middle of the screen to activate Reachability.

Given that you've allowed Reachability, you can enable the feature within any application by swiping down on the horizontal part, also called the home feature, at the bottom of your screen. There is no home pub on the home screen; nevertheless, you can still activate

Reachability on the home screen by swiping down from underneath the middle of the screen where you'll typically find the home feature.

How to Change Between & Force Quit Apps

You would find two various ways to change between applications on the iPhone 11: with the App Switcher and without. You can gain access to the App Switcher on the iPhone 11, 11 Pro and 11 Pro Max, by partly swiping upwards from underneath the screen. You can even switch between applications by swiping the home bar still left or right.

How to Open up the App Switcher on the iPhone

- Swipe halfway up from underneath the screen.

- Lift your finger, and the App Switcher would open up. You can swipe through, much like previous models, and touch on an application to open up it.

- To eliminate an application from App Switcher, swipe through to the app.

To switch applications without starting the App Switcher:

- Place your finger on the home bar or underneath the middle of the screen if the home button is absent.

- Swipe from left to open up your latest applications in descending order.

How to Switch OFF Power & Perform a Hard Restart

The Home button was central to numerous functions, including powering down your iPhone or forcing a hard restart whenever your iPhone freeze. To shut down or push a hard reset on the iPhone 11, 11 Pro, and 11 Pro Max, you would have to perform new gestures that involve a mixture of the medial side and Volume Up buttons.

To turn from the iPhone 11, 11 Pro and 11 Pro Max:

- Hold down the medial side button and the Volume Up or Down button before the option to slip to power off shows up.

- Using the Slip to Force Off toggle, swipe to the right.

You can even switch off the iPhone 11, iPhone 11 Pro, and iPhone 11 Pro Max from the overall portion of the Settings app.

- Open up the Settings application and choose *General*.

- Scroll entirely down to underneath, and tap TURN OFF.

- Glide to power icon to turn the power off.

You are capable of doing a hard restart, sometimes called a force shutdown, on your iPhone 11, iPhone 11 Pro, and iPhone 11 Pro Max. To execute a hard reboot:

- Quickly press and release the Volume Up accompanied by the Volume Down button.

- Now, press and maintain the side button before the device shuts down, and the Apple logo design appears.

- Your iPhone would automatically restart.

It's good to notice that whenever performing a hard Restart, it requires the iPhone 11 a couple of seconds to turn off when you're pressing the medial side button. So don't quit! I thought it wasn't working initially, but I needed to sustain the side button pressed down for a longer length of time.

How to Temporarily Disable Face ID

Face ID is not a perfect system; users have reported that some family members have had the opportunity to use cell phones protected Face ID due to a strong family resemblance. To briefly disable Face ID, you would have to keep down the medial side and Volume Up control keys to talk about the turn off-screen, and then tap Cancel to Force your iPhone to require the passcode to unlock briefly.

Here's how to briefly disable *Face ID* on the iPhone 11, 11 Pro and 11 Pro Max:

- Hold down the Volume Up or Down button and the medial side button simultaneously.

- After the shutdown screen appears, forget about the buttons. That is important; if you keep up to carry down the control keys, Emergency SOS would automatically be brought on.

- Touch the X at the bottom to cancel the shutdown.

Now, Face ID is briefly handicapped until you enter your passcode. Once you enter your passcode, Face ID would continue working as typical.

Chapter 19

iPhone 11 Face ID Secret Features

Reduce Alarm Volume and Keep Screen Brightness with Attention Awareness

Because Face ID can show when you're taking a look at your iPhone's screen, it can make your iPhone respond with techniques that produce sense predicated on your attention. You need to ensure that the interest Aware Features option is geared up by pursuing these steps:

- Tap _Settings_.

- Tap _Face ID & Passcode_.

- Type in your _passcode._

- Move the interest Aware Features slider to ON/Green

When you do this:

- **_When you have an alarm going off_**: and also you go through the screen, the volume of the alarm will automatically lower because the telephone knows it got your attention.

- ***The screen won't dim to save lots of battery***: Normally, the screen automatically dims after a brief period, if the telephone sees you are looking at the screen, it understands you're utilizing it and that you would like to start to see the screen.

Get Notification Previews Without Notification Centre

Typically, viewing full previews of notifications delivered to you by applications requires starting the *Notification Centre*. Not with Face ID. Since Face ID identifies you and unlocks your mobile phone, there is no risk that another person is viewing your private content. Due to that, changing your notification configurations can provide you with full notification previews without starting the Notification Centre. Here's how:

- Tap *Settings*.

- Touch *Notifications*.

- Touch *Show Previews*.

- Touch When Unlocked

Now, when you get a notification on your lock screen, take a look at your telephone (but don't swipe through to the screen to unlock it). When Face ID identifies you, the notification will rise to show the entire preview.

Autofill Passwords in Browser

The Autofill is your password as it pertains to authorizing payments or unlocking your phone with Face ID. Do you realize you can also utilize it to log into websites in Browser on the iPhone 11?

That is right: if you store your usernames and passwords in Browser to be auto-filled when you come to login screens, Face ID keeps your that data secure and functional only by you. Some tips about what you must do:

- *Save website usernames and passwords in the*

Browser when you log in to the sites by touching the pop-up menu.

- *Enable Face ID* to autofill those usernames and passwords by going to *Settings -> Face ID & Passcode -> enter your passcode -> moving the Browser Autofill slider to On/Green.*

- Visit a website where you have a merchant account preserved in Browser and go directly to the login screen.

- Touch the username or password field.

- Above the Browser keyboard, touch Passwords.

- In the menu that arises from underneath, touch an individual account you want to use.

- When the facial ID icon appears on the screen, position your iPhone 11 to scan that person. When Face ID authenticates you, your security password is added.

- Log in to the website.

Control Which Apps Can Gain access to Face ID

Every app that would require that you sign in would want to use Face ID since it's faster and better. Your real face scans aren't distributed to the applications (Apple converts the facial scan into an _abstract code_, so there is no risk that any applications could steal that info). Nevertheless, you might not want every app to have that access to (you can control how many other data applications can gain access too). If not, here's how to regulate which apps gain access to Face ID:

- Tap _Settings._

- Touch _Face ID & Passcode._

- Get into your passcode.

- Tap Other Apps

This screen lists all the applications installed on your iPhone that are looking to use Face ID. To stop apps from being able to access it, move the slider next to these to Off/white.

Switch OFF Face ID Quickly with Buttons

If you're in times where you come to mind that you may be required to use Face ID to unlock your mobile phone and reveal your data-for instance, during a conversation with the authorities or when crossing country borders-you may choose to switch off Face ID. And if time is vital in these circumstances, you would want to do it fast. Listed below are two ways to carefully turn off Face ID by pressing control keys on the iPhone 11:

- At the same time, press and contain the side button on the right of the telephone and either volume button (or both, if you like. Either works); this goes to the Shut down/Emergency screen. Face ID is currently off and also to unlock the telephone; you would be prompted to enter your passcode.

- Press the medial side button five times in quick succession; this causes the Emergency SOS feature, which brings deafening siren audio with it, so be ready for that. Touch Cancel on the Emergency SOS screen and then touch Stop Calling to get rid of the decision and the siren. Face ID is currently off.

Use Siri to Turn Off Face ID carefully

In addition to all or any of the other activities Siri can do, it may switch off Face ID for you. That is helpful for quickly turning off Face ID in the situations described earlier. You must have *"Hey Siri"* allowed for this feature to work, but if you need to do, here's what you must do:

- Without unlocking your telephone, tell it, "Hey Siri, whose telephone is this?"

- Siri will screen whatever info they have about you- generally a name, picture, plus some contact information (unless you want to buy even to show this, remove that from the Address Publication). At the same time, Face ID has been disabled.

- Now, to unlock the telephone or to change Face ID

on-again, enter your passcode.

Make Face ID Unlock Faster

Feel just like Face ID takes too much time to identify you and unlock your iPhone? You can speed up the procedure by tweaking:

- Touch *Settings*.

- Touch *Face ID & Passcode*.

- Insert your password.

- Move the *Require Attention for Face ID* slider to Off/white

This boosts *Face ID* speed, but it additionally makes your phone less secure. The *Require Attention* ensures that you are looking at the iPhone and also have your eyes open up for Face ID to unlock your mobile phone. By turning it off, things go faster; however, your telephone could be unlocked even if you are asleep, unconscious, or attempting not to adhere to someone wanting to pressure you to unlock your mobile phone.

Keep that risk at heart as you select whether to improve the settings.

Improve Face ID Accuracy

If Face ID doesn't recognize you and the passcode screen appears, enter your passcode immediately; when you do this, Face ID requires the checking of that person it didn't authorize. Adding the new check to the initial, it identifies that person from more perspectives and in more situations.

Face ID eventually throws these short-term matches out because they're not the area of the original, authoritative checkout. But, for some time, they help Face ID work a little much better.

If Face ID often does not identify you correctly, you almost certainly want to create it up again with a fresh face check by going through the process: *Configurations -> Face ID & Passcode -> enter your passcode -> Reset Face ID and then manage it again.*

Chapter 20

iPhone 11 Gestures You Should Know

Just like the iPhone 7 launched in 2017, the iPhone 11 doesn't include a physical home button, instead deciding on gestures to regulate the new user interface. It would require a couple of days to get used to the change but stay with it. By day three, you'll question how you ever coped without it, and using an "old" iPhone would appear old and antiquated.

1. **Unlock your iPhone 11:** Go through the phone and swipe up from underneath the screen. It truly is that easy, and also you don't need to hold back for the padlock icon at the very top to improve to the unlock visual before swiping up.

2. **Touch to wake:** Tap on your iPhone 11 screen when it's off to wake it up and find out what notifications you have. To unlock it with FaceID, you'll still have to set it up.

3. **Back to the Homescreen:** Whatever application

you are in, if you would like to return to the Home screen, swipe up from underneath of the screen. If you're within an application that is operating scenery, you'll need to keep in mind slipping up from underneath the screen (i.e., the medial side) rather than where the Home button used to be.

4. **Have a screenshot:** Press the power button and the volume up button together quickly, and it would snap a screenshot of whatever is on the screen.

5. **Addressing Control Centre:** It used to be always a swipe up, now it's a swipe down from the very best right of the screen. Even if your iPhone doesn't have 3D Touch, you can still long-press on the symbols to gain usage of further configurations within each icon.

6. **Accessing open up apps:** Previously, you raise tapped on the home button to uncover what apps you'd open. You now swipe up and then pause with your finger on the screen. After that, you can

see the applications you have opened up in the order you opened them.

7. **<u>Launch Siri</u>**: When you may use the "Hey Siri" hot term to awaken Apple's digital associate, there are still ways to release the function utilizing a button press. Press and contain the wake/rest button on the right aspect of the phone before Siri interface pops-up on screen.

8. **<u>Switch your phone off</u>**: Because long-pressing the wake/rest button launches Siri now, there's a fresh way for switching the phone off. To take action, you would need to press and contain the wake/rest button and the volume down button at the same time. Now glide to power off.

9. **<u>Release Apple Pay</u>**: Again, the wake/rest button is the main element here. Double touch it, and it would talk about your Apple Budget, then scan that person, and it'll request you to keep your phone near to the payment machine.

10. **<u>Gain access to widgets on the lock screen</u>**: Swipe

from still left to directly on your lock screen, ideal for checking your activity bands.

Using Memoji

- **<u>Create your Memoji</u>:** Open up Messages and begin a new meaning. Touch the tiny monkey icon above the keypad, and then strike the "+" button to generate your personality. You would customize face form, skin tone, curly hair colour, eye, jewellery, plus much more.

- **<u>Use your Memoji/Animoji in a FaceTime call</u>:** Take up a FaceTime call, then press the tiny star icon underneath the corner. Now, tap the Memoji you want to use.

- **<u>Memoji your selfies</u>:** So, if you select your Memoji face, preferably to your real to life face, you can send selfies with the Memoji changing your head in Messages. Take up a new message and touch the camera icon, and then press that top button. Now choose the Animoji option by tapping that monkey's mind again. Choose your Memoji and tap the '*X*,' not the "done" button, and then take your picture.

- **Record a Memoji video:** Sadly, Memoji isn't available as a choice in the camera app, but that doesn't mean you can't record one. Much like the picture selfie, go to communications, touch on the camera icon and then slip to video and then tap on the superstar. Weight the Animoji or your Memoji, and off you decide to go.

iOS 13 iPhone 11 Notification Tips

- *Notifications collection to provide quietly*: If you're worried that you would be getting way too many notifications, you can place the way they deliver with an app by application basis. Swipe left when you've got a notification on the Lock screen and touch on Manage. Touch Deliver Quietly. Calm notifications come in Notification Centre, but do not show up on the Lock screen, play audio, present a banner or badge the application icon.

You've just surely got to be sure you check every once in a while.

- *Switch off notifications from an app*: Same method as the "Deliver Quietly" feature, other than you tap the "Switch off..." option.

- *Open up Notification Centre on Lock screen*: From your lock screen, swipe up from the center of the screen, and you would visit a long set of earlier notifications if you have any.

- *Check Notifications anytime*: To check on your Notifications anytime, swipe down from the very best left part of the screen to reveal them.

Using Screen Time

- *Checking your Screen Time*: You can examine how you've been making use of your phone with the new Screen Time feature in iOS 13. You'll find the reviews in *Configurations > Screen Time*.

- *Scheduled Downtime:* If you want just a little help

making use of your mobile phone less, you can restrict what applications you utilize when. Check out Settings > Screen Time and choose the Downtime option. Toggle the change to the "on" position and choose to routine a period when only specific applications and calls are allowed. It's ideal for preventing you or your children from using their cell phones after an arranged time, for example.

- *Set application limits*: App Limitations enable you to choose which group of applications you want to include a period limit to. Choose the category and then "add" before choosing a period limit and striking "plans."

- *Choose "always allowed" apps*: However, you might be willing to lock down your phone to avoid you utilizing it, that's no good if most of your way of getting in touch with people is via an application that gets locked away. Utilize this feature always to allow certain applications whatever limitations you apply.

- *Content & Personal privacy limitations*: This section is also within the primary Screen Time configurations menu and particularly useful if you are a mother or father with kids who use iOS devices. Utilizing it, you can restrict all types of content and options, including iTunes and in-app buys, location services, advertising, etc. It's worth looking at.

Siri shortcuts

- *Siri Shortcuts*: There are several little "help" the iPhone 11 offers via Siri Shortcuts. To start to see the ones recommended for you, go to *Configurations > Siri & Search* and choose what you think would be helpful from the automatically produced suggestions. Touch "all shortcuts" to see more. If you wish to install specific "shortcuts" for a variety of different applications that aren't recommended by the iPhone, you can do this by downloading the dedicated Siri Shortcuts.

iPhone 11 Control Centre Tips

- *Add new handles*: Just like the previous version of iOS, you can include and remove handles from Control Centre. Check out *Configurations > Control Centre > Customize Handles* and then choose which settings you would like to add.

- *Reorganize handles*: To improve the order of these settings, you've added, touch, and contain the three-bar menu on the right of whichever control you would like to move, then move it along the list to wherever you would like it to be.

- *Expand handles*: Some settings may become full screen, press harder on the control you want to expand, and it will fill the screen.

- *Activate screen recording*: Among the new options, you can include regulating Centre is Screen Recording. Be sure you add the control, then open up Control Centre and press the icon that appears like an excellent white circle in the thin white band. To any extent further, it'll record everything that occurs on your screen. Press the control again if you are done, and it will save a video to your Photos application automatically.

- ***Adjust light/screen brightness***: You can activate your camera adobe flash, utilizing it as a torch by starting Control Centre and tapping on the torch icon. If you wish to adjust the lighting, power press the icon, then adapt the full-screen slider that shows up.

- ***Quickly switch where a sound is played***: One cool feature is the capability to change where music is playing. While music is playing, through Apple Music, Spotify, or wherever, press on the music control or touch the tiny icon in the very best part of the music control; this introduces a pop-up screening available devices that you can play through; this may be linked earphones, a Bluetooth loudspeaker, Apple Television, your iPhone, or any AirPlay device.

- ***Set an instant timer***: Rather than going to the

timer app, you can force press on the timer icon, then glide up or down on the full-screen to create a timer from about a minute to two hours long.

- ***How to gain access to HomeKit devices***: Open up Control Centre and then tap on the tiny icon that appears like a home.

iPhone 11 Photos and Camera Tips

- ***Enable/disable Smart HDR***: Among the new iPhone's camera advancements is HDR, which helps boost colors, light, and detail in hard light conditions. It's on by default, but if you would like to get it turned on or off, you manually can check out *Settings > Camera and discover the Smart HDR toggle change.*

- ***Keep a standard photograph with HDR***: Right under the Smart HDR toggle is a "Keep Normal Photo" option, which would save a regular, no HDR version of your picture as well as the Smart

HDR photo.

- *Portrait Lights*: To take Portrait Setting shots with artificial lights, first go to capture in Family portrait mode. Portrait Setting only works for people on the iPhone 11 when capturing with the rear-facing camera. To choose your Portrait Setting capturing style, press and hang on the screen where it says "DAYLIGHT" and then move your finger to the right.

- *Edit Portrait Lights after taking pictures*: Open up any Family portrait shot in Photos and then tap "edit." After another or two, you will see the light effect icon at the bottom of the image, touch it, and swipe just as you did when shooting the picture.

- *Edit Portrait setting Depth*: Using the new iPhone 11, you can modify the blur impact after shooting the Portrait shot. Check out Photos and choose the picture you want to regulate, then select "edit." You will see a depth slider at the bottom of the screen. Swipe to boost the blur strength, swipe left to diminish it.

- *How exactly to Merge People in Photos app*: Photos in iOS can check out your photos and identify people and places. If you discover that the application has chosen the same person, but says they vary, you can combine the albums collectively. To get this done, go directly to the Photos application > Albums and choose People & Places. Touch on the term "Select" at the very top right of the screen and then select the images of individuals you want to merge, then tap "merge."

- *Remove people in Photos app*: Head to Photos App, Albums, and choose People & Places. To eliminate tap on "Choose" and then tap on individuals, you do not want to see before tapping on "Remove" underneath still left of your iPhone screen.

iPhone 11: Keyboard Tips

- ***Go one-handed***: iOS 13's QuickType keypad enables you to type one-handed, which is fantastic on the larger devices like the iPhone 11 and XS Greatest extent. Press and contain the emoji or world icon and then keypad configurations. Select either the still left or right-sided keypad. It shrinks the keyboard and techniques it to 1 aspect of the screen. Get back to full size by tapping the tiny arrow.

- ***Use your keyboard as a trackpad***: Previously, with 3D Touch shows, you utilize the keyboard area as a trackpad to go the cursor on the screen. You'll still can, but it works just a little in a different way here, rather than pressure pressing anywhere on the keypad, press, and hangs on the spacebar instead.

Face ID Tips

- *Adding another in-person ID*: if you regularly change appearance now, you can put in a second In person ID to state the iPhone 11 getting puzzled. That is also really useful if you would like to add your lover to allow them to use your mobile phone while you're traveling, for example.

iPhone 11: Screen Tips

- *Standard or Zoomed screen*: Since iPhone 6 Plus, you've had the opportunity to select from two quality options. You can transform the screen settings from Standard or Zoomed on the iPhone 11 too. To change between your two - if you have changed your mind after set up - go to *Configurations* > *Screen & Lighting* > *Screen Focus and choose Standard or Zoomed.*

- *Enable True Tone screen*: If you didn't get it done

at the step, you could transform it anytime. To get the iPhone's screen to automatically change its color balance and heat to complement the background light in the area, check out Control Centre and push press the screen lighting slider. Now touch the True Firmness button. You can even go to *Configurations > Screen and Lighting and toggle the "True Shade" switch.*

iPhone 11 Battery Tips

- *Check your average battery consumption*: In iOS 13, you can check out Settings > Battery, and you will see two graphs. One shows the electric battery level; the other shows your screen on and screen off activity. You would find two tabs. One shows your last day; the other turns up to fourteen days; this way, you can view how energetic your phone battery strength and breakdowns screening your average screen on and off times show under the graphs.

- *Enable Low-Power Mode*: The reduced Power

Mode (Settings > Electric battery) enables you to reduce power consumption. The feature disables or lessens background application refresh, auto-downloads, email fetch, and more (when allowed). You can turn it on at any point, or you are prompted to carefully turn it on at the 20 and 10 % notification markers. You can even put in control to regulate Centre and get access to it quickly by swiping up to gain access to Control Centre and tapping on the electric battery icon.

- *Find electric battery guzzling apps*: iOS specifically lets you know which apps are employing the most power. Head to Configurations > Electric battery and then scroll right down to the section that provides you with an in-depth look at all of your battery-guzzling apps.

- *Check your battery via the Electric battery widget*: Inside the widgets in Today's view, some cards enable you to start to see the battery life staying in your iPhone, Apple Watch, and linked headphones. Just swipe from left to directly on your Home screen to access your Today view and scroll until you start to see the "Batteries" widget.

- *Charge wirelessly*: To utilize the iPhone's wifi charging capabilities, buy a radio charger. Any Qi charger will continue to work, but to charge more effectively, you will need one optimized for Apple's 7.5W charging.

- *Fast charge it*: When you have a 29W, 61W, or 87W USB Type-C power adapter for a MacBook, you can plug in your iPhone 11 Pro utilizing a Type-C to Lightning wire watching it charge quickly. Up to 50 % in thirty minutes.

Chapter 21

How to Group Applications

Creating folders on your iPhone is a sensible way to reduce mess on your home screen. Grouping apps collectively can also make it simpler to use your phone - if all your music applications are in the same place, you would not have to be searching through folders or looking at your mobile phone when you wish to utilize them.

How you create folders isn't immediately apparent, but once you understand the secret, it's simple — some tips about what you should know about how to make a folder on your iPhone.

How to Create Folders and Group Apps on the iPhone

- To make a folder, you will need at least two applications to place into the folder. Determine which two you want to use.

- Gently touch and hold one of the applications until all applications on the screen start shaking (this is the same process that you utilize to re-arrange apps).

  NOTE: Making folders on the iPhone 6S and 7 series, the iPhone 8 and iPhone X, and iPhone 11 Pro and 11, is just a little trickier. That's because the 3D Touchscreen on those models responds differently to different presses on the screen. When you have one particular cell phones, don't press too much or you'll result in a menu or shortcut. Only a light touch and hold will do.

- Pull one of the applications at the top of the other. When the first application appears to merge into the second one, take your finger from the screen. Dropping one form into the other creates the folder.

- What goes on next depends upon what version of the iOS you're working with or using.

- In iOS 7 and higher, the folder and its own recommended name take up the whole screen.

- In iOS 4-6, you Typically the two applications and a name for the folder in a strip over the screen

- Every folder has a name assigned to it by default (more on this in a moment); nevertheless, you can transform that name by touching the x icon to clear the recommended name and then type the name you want.

- If you wish to add more applications to the folder, touch the wallpaper to close the folder. Then pull more apps into the new folder.

- When you've added all the applications you want

and edited the name, click on the Home button on the leading Centre of the iPhone as well as your changes would be saved (precisely like when re-arranging icons).

TIPS: *When you have an iPhone 11, 11 Pro, or newer, there is no Home button to click. Instead, you should tap* **Done** *on the right part of the screen.*

How Default iPhone Folder Titles Are Suggested

When you initially create a folder, the iPhone assigns a suggested name to it. That name is chosen predicated on the App Store category that the applications in the folder result from; for instance if the applications result from the Video games category, the recommended name of the folder is Video games. You should use the suggested name or add your own using the instructions in steps above.

How to Edit Folders on Your iPhone

If you have already created a folder on your iPhone, you

might edit it by changing the name, adding or removing apps, and more. Here's how:

- To edit a pre-existing folder, touch and hold the folder until it starts to move.

- Touch it another time, and the folder will open up, and its material will fill up the screen.

- You may make the next changes

  ▪ Edit the folder's name by tapping on the written text.

  ▪ Add more applications by dragging them in.

  ▪ Remove applications from the folder by dragging them away.

- Click on the Home button or the Done button to save lots of your changes.

How to Remove Apps From Folders on iPhone

If you wish to remove an application from a folder on your iPhone or iPod touch, follow these steps:

- Touch and hold the folder that you would like to eliminate the application from.

- When the applications and folders start wiggling, remove your finger from the screen.

- Touch the folder you want to eliminate the application.

- Drag the application from the folder and onto the home screen.

- Click on the Home or Done button to save lots of the new set up.

How to Add Folders to the iPhone Dock

The four applications over the bottom of the iPhone reside in what's called the Dock. You can include folders to the dock if you'd like. To achieve that:

- Move one of the applications currently in the dock away by tapping, keeping, and dragging it to the primary section of the home screen.

- Move a folder into space.

- Press the Home or Done button, depending on your iPhone model, to save lots of the change.

How to Delete a Folder on the iPhone

Deleting a folder is comparable to eliminating an app. Some tips about what you must do:

- Pull all the applications from the folder and onto the home screen.

- When you do that, the folder disappears.

- Press the home or Done button to save lots of the change, and you're done.

Chapter 22

15 Recommended iPhone Applications

<u>Spark</u>: Best Email App for iPhone 11

If you centre on iOS apps, you would understand that email has taken on something similar to the role of the antagonist in the wonderful world of iOS. App designers appear to know that everyone needs a better email platform, and they want an application to resolve their issues. Controlling email is just a little less stressful if you are using *Spark* as you would find features to suit your needs, such as; sending, snoozing email messages, and a good inbox that only notifies you of important email messages.

Below are the things you'd like about this application:

- The app is simple to use and socially friendly.

- Swipe-based interaction allows for one-handed operation.

What You may not like about it:

- No filter systems for automatically sorting email messages.

- The app does not have a way of controlling messages in batches.

Things: *The best "To-do manager" for the iPhone 11*

To-do manager applications are a packed field, and the application called *"Things"* isn't the only good one, and it is also not the only *to-do manager* on this list, but it's a carefully reliable tool, seated between control and hardy. The application provides the ideal levels of both control and hardy, without mind-boggling users to dials and without dropping essential features.

Things you'd like about this application:

- This app has a simplified interface that reduces stress when adding and completing the task.

- Tasks can be added from iOS with the sheet extension.

What you may not like are:

- Repeating tasks and deadlines can be buggy.

- Tasks can't be put into the calendar automatically.

<u>OmniCentre</u>: Best GTD-compatible To-Do App for iPhone 11

Like *"Things," OmniCentre* is a favourite and well-designed to-do manager; however, they have a different group of priorities. Where *Things* attempts to remain simple and straightforward, *OmniCentre* is feature-rich and robust.

The application fully integrates with the *"Getting Things Done"* approach to task management called **GTD**, and this method stimulates users to jot down any duties they have, as well as almost all their associated information and scheduling. GTD users would finish up spending a great deal of time on leading end arranging work; because of this, the software takes a robust feature collection to implement all areas of the GTD process.

Things you'd like about this application:

- Most effective to-do list manager available.

- Can participate in virtually any task management style.

What you may not like:

- Sacrifices simpleness and usability for power and versatility.

<u>*Agenda*</u>*: Best iPhone 11 App for Busy Notice Takers*

Agenda requires a different spin on the notes application than almost every other application; its also known as *"date centred notice taking app."* Records are structured by task and day, and the times are a large part of the Agenda. Instead of merely collecting your jotting into a collection, Agenda creates a to-do list from *"things,"* with tight time integration, Agenda makes an operating journaling app and an able to-do manager and general iPhone 11 note-taking app. The day and note mixture seems apparent, but Agenda is the first iOS note-taking application to perform this mixture effectively.

It's a "to-do manager" and also a note-taking application with some calendar features, which enables seeing every information in a single place with one perspective and only one app. The application is also highly practical in the freeform, which may be uncommon in flagship apps. The beauty of the app *"Agenda"* comes out when using Pencil support, but for the present time, we'll have to turn to the iPad Pro for the feature.

Things you'd like about this application:

- Note-taking small tweaks can improve many workflows.

- The time-based organization fits most users; mental types of information organization.

What you may not like:

- Slow app release can limit how quickly you can write down a note.

1Password: Best iPhone 11 App for Security password Management

Using the auto-fill in iOS 13, *1Password* is as near to perfect as we have in a password manager. The Face ID authentication isn't unique to the iPhone 11 alone, but access Face ID makes the application better and simpler to use, which is an uncommon combination of accomplishments to reach concurrently.

Things you'd like about this application:

- Finding and copying usernames and passwords is extremely easy.

- Secure document storage space means *1Password* can gather all of your secure information in a single place.

- Auto-fill support finally makes security password management as easy as typing your security password.

What you may not like:

- No free version.

- The paid version uses membership pricing.

Twitterific: Best Tweets App For iPhone 11

Twitter is probably not the most exceptional sociable media system, but it's still one of the very most popular internet sites around, and like many internet sites, Twitter's default application is disappointingly bad.

Unfortunately, Twitter does lately nerf third-party Twitter clients. Third-party applications won't receive real-time stream notifications, significantly reducing the effectiveness of the applications; this move seems to pressure users to go to the native app, but considering its many defects, Twitterific and applications like it remain better.

Things you'd like about this application:

- Improves Twitter's visual demonstration dramatically.

- Includes smart and powerful features that make Twitter simpler to use.

What you may not like:

- Some organizational options are initially unintuitive.

- Twitter has purposefully knee-capped a good number of third-party apps, and Twitterific is no defence to those results.

Overcast: *Best iPhone 11 App for Podcasts*

Overcast is the best application you may use to hear podcasts. The app's user interface is considered carefully for maximal consumer performance, with features like "Smart Rate" which helps to intelligently manages a podcast's playback speed to shorten silences without accelerating speech, while Tone of voice Boost offers a pre-built EQ curve made to amplify voices, which is ideal for a loud hearing environment.

Things you'd like about this application:

- Thoughtfully designed interface for sorting and hearing podcasts.

- Features like Smart Speed and Queue playlists are invaluable once you're used to them.

- Active developer centred on avoiding an unhealthy user experience concerning monetization.

What you may not like;

- It most definitely doesn't seem to go nicely with the iOS lock screen.

Apollo: Best iPhone 11 App for Reddit

If you're thinking about *Reddit*, you would want to see the website beyond the third-party app. The application has improved, sure, but it's still kilometres behind third-party offerings.

Apollo is the best of the number as it pertains to Reddit clients, conquering out past champions like "Narwhal." Development is continuous and ongoing, with many improvements from the dev in the app's subreddit.

The swipe-based navigation would continue to work on any iPhone, of course, but it dovetails nicely with the iPhone 11's application switching behaviour. The real black setting is also a delicacy for OLED screens.

Things you'd like about this application:

- Effortlessly handles an enormous variety of media.

- Well developed UI makes navigation easy.

- No ads in virtually any version of the app.

What you may not like:

- Sometimes is suffering from annoying and lingering bugs.

Focos: *Best iPhone 11 App for Editing and enhancing Portrait Setting Photos*

By default, the iPhone 11's Family portrait Mode is a one-and-done process; you take the picture, and the blur is applied. iOS doesn't give a built-in way for editing and enhancing the Picture Setting effect following the fact. Focos fills the space, creating a tool to tweak both degrees of shadow and the blur face mask. It mimics the result you'd see when modifying a zoom lens' physical aperture. More magically, you can also change the centre point following the shot by recreating the blurred cover up on the different object, or by hand adjusting the result on the image's depth face mask instantly.

Things you'd like about this application:

- The most effective approach to manipulating Portrait Mode's depth-of-field effect.

- The depth map is a distinctive feature to help visualize blur.

What you may not like:

- Simple to make images look over-processed.

- Only about the centre, 50% of the blur range looks natural.

Halide: Best iPhone 11 App for Natural Photos

Distinctively, *Halide* sticks essential info in the iPhone 11's "ear." It embeds a live histogram for image evaluation; could it be precious? Nearly, but Halide is a near-perfect picture taking software besides that offering feature.

The settings are ideally positioned and configured, the RAW catch is pixel-perfect, and navigation within the application is easy and immediately understandable. If you are seriously interested in taking photos on your iPhone 11, *Halide* is the best camera application for iOS.

Things you'd like about this application:

- Low handling power for iPhone photos.

- The broadest toolset of any iOS image editing and enhancing the app.

What you may not like:

- It can overwhelm first-time users using its degree

of control.

Euclidean Lands: The Top-rated AR Puzzle Game for iPhone 11

Augmented reality applications haven't yet found their killer use. But AR gambling takes great benefit from lots of the iPhone 11's features.

Euclidean Lands is a short fun puzzler that calls for the full benefit of AR's potential. Similar to Monument Valley, players manipulate the play space to produce new pathways through puzzle designs, guiding their avatar to the finish of the maze. The overall game begins easy; nevertheless, you might be scratching your head just a little by the end.

Things you'd like in this application:

- Challenging and attractive puzzle levels that take benefit of AR's unique features.

What you may not like:

- Disappointingly short.

- The core game auto technician feels very familiar.

Giphy World: Best AR Messaging App for iPhone 11

Plenty of applications have tried to usurp Snapchat as an AR messaging system. While Snapchat might maintain a weakened condition because of self-inflicted damage, it isn't eliminated yet. But if it can decrease, Giphy World is a great replacement.

Things you'd like about this application:

- Simple to create fun and funny images from provided assets.

- Content isn't locked inside the Giphy app.

What you may not like:

- Object place and processing speed are inferior compared to Snapchat's.

Jig Space: Best Usage of AR for Education on iPhone

11

Learning with holograms is one particular thing you regularly see in sci-fi movies; with ***Jig Space*** and ***augmented*** actuality, that kind of thing is now possible in our daily lives. You should use the application to find out about various topics, including what sort of lock works, manipulating every part of the system, and looking at it from alternative perspectives. Jig Space requires the benefit of AR's three sizes effectively, and the low-poly models AR has bound not to harm the grade of the visualizations.

Things you'd like about this application:

- Takes benefit of AR's advantages for a good cause.

- A substantial assortment of "jigs" charges is free.

What you may not like:

- Accompanying captions are occasionally disappointingly shallow.

Nighttime Sky: Best Late-Night Outside Companion

App

Directing out constellations is much more fun if you are not making them up as you decide to go. *Evening Sky* was the main augmented-reality style application to seem on iOS. It shows just how for others on the system wanting to mimic its success, but it's remained dominant nevertheless.

Things you'd like about this application:

- It enhances the natural world with technology.

- It improves the star-gazing experience for both children and adults.

What you may not like:

- Large image units mean large camera motions are stiff and jerky.

Inkhunter: Most Readily Useful AR Gimmick on iOS

There's something distinctively exotic about checking out new tattoos by yourself. *Inkhunter* uses the energy of augmented truth to generate short-term digital symbols you can construct on the body and screenshot. You should use the built-in adobe flash, pull your designs, or import property from somewhere else to project on your skin.

Things you'd like about this application:

- Fun and book application idea that's useful.

What you may not like:

- Is suffering from AR's existing restrictions in surface matching.

Chapter 23

How to Restart an iPhone (All Models)

The iPhone is a robust computer that ties in a pocket. As being a pc or laptop, sometimes an iPhone must be restarted or reset to repair a problem. To restart an iPhone, transform it off, then transform it on. When an iPhone doesn't react to a restart, execute a reset. Neither process deletes the info or configurations on the iPhone. These aren't exactly like a restore, which erases all this content on the iPhone and returning it to manufacturing conditions, and you restore your computer data from a back-up.

How to Restart the iPhone X, iPhone 11 Pro, iPhone 11, and iPhone 8 (Plus)

Restart an iPhone to resolve fundamental problems, such as poor cellular or Wi-Fi connectivity, application crashes, or other day-to-day glitches. On these models, Apple designated new functions to the *Rest/Wake button* privately of these devices. It could be used to activate *Siri*, talk about the Emergency SOS feature, or other tasks. As a result of this change, the restart process differs from the technique used in previous models.

To restart an iPhone 11, iPhone X, and iPhone 8:

- Press and contain the Rest/Wake and Volume Down buttons at the same time. Volume up works, too, but utilizing it can unintentionally have a screenshot.

- When the slide to power off slider shows up, release the Rest/Wake and Volume Down buttons.

- Move the slider from left to shut down the phone.

How to Restart Other iPhone Models

Restarting other iPhone models is equivalent to turning the iPhone On/Off. Some tips about what to do:

- ***Press and contain the Rest/Wake button***: On old models, it's at the top of the phone. On the iPhone 6 series and newer, it's on the right part.

- When the power off slider appears on the screen, release the Rest/Wake button.

- *Move the power off slider from left to right*: This gesture prompts the iPhone to turn off. A spinner shows on the screen indicating the shutdown is happening. It might be dim and hard to see.

- When the phone shuts off, press and contain the *Rest/Wake button*.

- When the Apple logo design appears on the screen, release the *Sleep/Wake button*, and await the iPhone to complete restarting.

How to Precisely Hard Reset the iPhone 11, iPhone X and iPhone 8

The essential restart solves many problems, but it generally does not answer all of them. In a few cases, such as when the phone is completely freezing and won't react to pressing the Rest/Wake button, a better option called a *hard reset* is necessary.

On iPhone 11, iPhone X, and iPhone 8 series, the hard reset process differs from other models. To hard reset these iPhone models:

- Click and release the Volume Up button.

- Click and release the Volume down button.

- Press and contain the Rest/Wake button before gliding to power off slider appears.

- Move the slip to force off slider from left to reset the phone.

How to Hard Reset Other iPhone Models

A hard reset restarts the phone and refreshes the memory space that applications run in. It generally does not delete data but usually helps the iPhone begin from scratch. Typically, a hard reset is not needed, however when it is necessary on a mature model (except iPhone 7), follow these steps:

- With the phone screen facing you, press down the Sleep/Wake button and the home button at the same time.

- Continue to contain the control keys when the power off slider shows up, don't release the control keys.

- When the Apple logo design appears, release the Sleep/Wake button and the home button.

- Wait as the iPhone resets.

How to Hard Reset iPhone 7 Series

The hard reset process is somewhat different for the iPhone 7 series. That's because the home button is not a physical button on these models; it's a 3D Touch -panel. Because of this, Apple transformed how these models are reset.

Using the iPhone 7 series, keep the Volume Down button pressed, and the Sleep/Wake button at the same time.

For more Help Resetting Your iPhone

Sometimes an iPhone may have problems so complicated a restart or reset doesn't work. Follow these advanced troubleshooting steps to fix the problem:

- **_Stuck at Apple Logo_**: If an iPhone is stuck at the Apple logo during startup, a straightforward restart might not be adequate to solve the problem. I recommend taking the iPhone to a professional or Apple repair centre.

- **_Restore to Manufacturing default Settings_**: If you wish to erase all the info from an iPhone and begin from inception, this solves some hard bugs. Before you sell your iPhone, restore it to factory settings.

- **_Recovery Setting_**: If an iPhone is stuck in a reboot loop or can't see through the Apple logo design during startup, try iPhone recovery mode.

- **_DFU Mode_**: When downgrading the version of the iOS or jailbreak the phone, use DFU (Disk Firmware Update) mode.

CHAPTER 24

The Quick Fix for iPhone 11 Phones

If you buy a used iPhone mobile, it is interesting. In the end, you come with an iPhone 11 Series (iPhone 11, iPhone 11 Pro, and iPhone 11 Pro Max) and stretch your budget by acquiring a used one, especially for individuals who are not economically buoyant.

Some individuals encounter this issue along the way of activating their new device: The iPhone 11 Series (iPhone 11, iPhone 11 Pro, and iPhone 11 Pro Max) will inquire further for somebody else's Apple ID and wouldn't typically work unless supplied.

This isn't a challenge that can't be fixed, so do not fret because you'll get it fixed following these steps.

- It is consequently an attribute of Apple's Find my iPhone 11 Series (iPhone 11, iPhone 11 Pro and iPhone 11 Pro Max) service known as activation lock.

- Activation Lock is a security measure that Apple raised to cope with the allergy of iPhone 11 Series (iPhone 11, iPhone 11 Pro, and iPhone 11 Pro

Max) thefts. In earlier years, if someone takes an iPhone 11 Series (iPhone 11, iPhone 11 Pro, and iPhone 11 Pro Max) without blockage by lock feature, they could clean it, resell it, and breakout with the crime. The activation lock altered the situation.

- When the initial owner setup finds my iPhone 11 Series (iPhone 11, iPhone 11 Pro, and iPhone 11 Pro Max) on the tool, the **Apple ID** used would be stored on Apple's activation servers together with almost every other information about the phone. The activation servers will most effectively unlock the phone again if that unique Apple ID can be used. If you no more have the Apple ID, you'll never be in a position to activate or use the phone. It facilitates the security of your iPhone 11 Series (iPhone 11, iPhone 11 Pro, and iPhone 11 Pro Max) because nobody would like to grab a phone they can't use. On the other hand, it generally does not harm you if you recently procure the phone.

- Dealing with the activation lock is annoying, but additionally, it is smooth to solve. It's mainly possible, and the prior consumer just forgot to carefully turn off find my iPhone 11 Series (iPhone 11, iPhone 11 Pro, and iPhone 11 Pro Max) or erase the tool correctly before offering it on the market (though it could also be a sign you've purchased a stolen device, so be cautious).

- You should contact the preceding owner of the telephone for him/her to consider the necessary steps.

How to Wipe an iPhone 11 Using iCloud

Imagine if you can't gain access to the vendor/merchant due to some reasons, yet you would need your mobile phone to be wiped entirely for easy convenience, the seller may use iCloud to erase it. This is attained by ensuring the phone you want to get triggered linked to a WiFi network or mobile data network, and then inform the seller to follow along with the next steps:

- Visit http://iCloud.com/#find
- Sign in with the Apple id he/she applied to the phone that is with you or sold to you.

- Click *All Devices*.

- Choose the phone sold you or available to you.

- Select *Erase iPhone*.

- When the phone is erased, click *Remove from Accounts*.

- Restart the phone, and you are all set.

How to Remove Activation Lock using iCloud

Sometimes, things can get a bit messy and complicated if the merchant/seller cannot physically access the phone, thanks to circumstances such as distance, among other factors. This may also be resolved effortlessly as the owner may use iCloud to eliminate the activation lock from the phone through his accounts by following the steps below:

- Visit *iCloud.com* on any device, either mobile or laptop.

- Log-on with the Apple ID he/she used to activate the telephone.

- Click Find My iPhone.

- Select All Devices.

- Go through the iPhone you sold or want to market.

- Select **Remove from Accounts.**

Having achieved that, after that, you can PULL THE PLUG ON the iPhone, and you switch it ON again. After that, you can proceed with the standard activation process.

How to Erase an iPhone 11 Using Find My iPhone App

This process is very much indeed identical to the approach explained above using iCloud by just using the Find my iPhone application installed on some other iPhone 11 Series (iPhone 11, iPhone 11 Pro, and iPhone 11 Pro Max) device. If the owner prefers to get this done, connect the phone you're buying to Wi-Fi or mobile data, and then inform the owner to adhere to the steps below:

- Start the *find my iPhone* app.

- Sign on with the Apple ID they applied to the phone sold

to you.

- Choose the phone.
- Tap *Actions*.
- Tap *Erase iPhone*.
- Tap *Erase iPhone* (It is the same button, however, on a new display).
- Enter *Apple ID*.
- Tap *Erase*.
- Tap *Remove from Accounts*.

Restart the iPhone and get started doing the setup process.

How to Remove Activation Lock on iPhone

- It is expedient that you should unlock or remove the activation lock from the acquired iPhone by inputting the prior owners' **Apple ID.** This technique can be initiated by getting in contact with the owner and detailing the scenario.

- If the owner lives near to you, I'll recommend that you hand over the phone back to him/her with the mission to insert the mandatory unlock code, which is his/her **Apple ID**. When the seller gets the iPhone at hand, he/she only will enter the necessary Apple ID on the activation lock display. Having done such, restart the telephone and then forge forward with the typical activation process.

Chapter 25

5 Differences Between iPhone 11 & iPhone X

Apple enthusiasts unite: Many long-anticipated Apple announcements were confirmed and unveiled throughout a live blast of the Apple event that was hosted by Apple CEO **Tim** at the Steve Careers Theater on Sept. 10. Among the many services and features that Apple revealed today, the facts about the new iPhone 11, like the differences between your iPhone 11 and iPhone X models, were possibly the most eagerly anticipated - and the young man did the meeting delivery.

Having a whole new conventional telephone is fun, but could it be worthwhile to ditch your iPhone X (or other older model) for only the shiny new iPhone 11? Well, Perhaps that depends on;

- how practical (or not) your present iPhone model is, and

- if the significant new iPhone 11 features pique your interest or not.

Thankfully, the facts shared in the live stream can make your decision-making a bit easier. Listed below are the five most significant variations between your iPhone X and the iPhone 11 that you will desire to be aware of before deciding if to trade in your old model, in conditions of colours, prices, camera work, and the rest of the major things which were announced. Take note, though, that is just evaluating the iPhone X to the iPhone 11, rather than the other two models which were also announced, the iPhone 11 Pro and iPhone 11 Pro Max, which you can find out about in this book.

1. *iPhone 11 comes in Six Fun, New Colours*

I'm one of these people who cares way too much about the colour of their iPhone's outside - why I had been such a sucker for both (now nearly-vintage) iPhone 5C and my iPhone XR model. With regards to the iPhone 11, we will have a much bigger collection of fun colours to choose from than we did with the iPhone X.

iPhone X came in merely two simple colour options - metallic and space grey. However, the new iPhone 11 comes in six fun colours: *Dark, white, crimson, green, yellowish, and red.* If you are someone who prefers to show off your particular flavour and personality through your phone colour choice, the iPhone 11 will give you a lot more opportunity to do this than the iPhone X.

2. *The iPhone 11 Camera has Some Major Upgrades*

Probably one of the most anticipated feature improvements as it pertains to any new iPhone unveiling involves anything regarding the camera - and iPhone 11's reported improvements do not disappoint. First of all, unlike the iPhone X (or any other previous model, for example), rather than 1X and 2X and the primary zoom options, nowadays, there are three, with ultra-wide represented as a "0.5x" or fifty percent focus. It's choice I find just a little complicated since Samsung describes its three capturing settings with a stand of trees and shrubs: one tree represents 2X, two represents no move and a relatively distant band of three trees and shrubs represents ultra-wide (I honestly can't decide which is more evident).

Even if you're not in the iPhone 11 Pro's new ultra-wide camera mode, the new camera application will always demonstrate the amount of visual information you're abandoning: the dark borders of the camera application turn translucent, and that means you can see the actual ultra-wide zoom lens, which would be added if you were utilizing it.

Apple, also, has introduced a Camera App drawer that you gain access to by swiping up close to the bottom level of the display. Under it, is aspect percentage *(4:3 or 16:9), Live photos, display, filters, HDR*, as well as your timer (I had been a little annoyed that Apple hid it this way). I love the new QuickTake video feature, which enables you to switch from picture set to video by just keeping down the shutter button. After that, you can slip it to them to lock it on while keeping the usage of a photo-in-video button on the right.

3. *There are a few Fun Video Updates, Too*

The camera's perks don't connect with photos alone, of course. There are a few r fun new video functions that come in handy - specifically for those folks who go on Instagram and Snapchat 24/7. First of all, based on the live stream, iPhone 11 gets the highest-quality video of any smartphone out there, so you are getting the best of the greatest.

One fun new feature called ***"QuickTake"*** gives you to efficiently record brief videos without turning toggles in your camera app. Keep down the picture shutter button (just like you'll when documenting a video within an Instagram tale), and you may take a brief video in the centre of a photo take, and never have to interrupt your circulation and switch to the individual video screen.

Another fun new feature is the capability to record slow-motion footage on leading facing cameras, leading to what Apple knew as a *"Slofie"* (or a slow-motion video selfie). Prepare to up your selfie game in sexy, dramatic, '80s-music-video-style techniques the iPhone X can't deliver.

4. *iPhone 11 has a Longer Electric Battery Life & Better Speed*

If you are someone who's continually chasing down chargers, excellent news - iPhone 11 is swooping directly in to help us make the majority of our phone's electric battery life by ensuring it's an extended one. Based on the Apple event, the iPhone 11's "all day long battery life" is longer than previous models - and you will be one hour longer than even the iPhone XR's battery life, which at the time had the most extended battery life of any smartphone.

Additionally, it's reported that the iPhone 11 will surpass the iPhone X as long as the effectiveness of both its central processing unit and graphics processing unit, as it possesses the quickest CPU and GPU of any smartphone on the marketplace; this bodes perfectly for the overall speed of the new iPhone and is especially helpful for operating mobile video games (perhaps via the freshly-announced Apple Arcade) if that's your glass o' tea.

5. *iPhone 11 is Cheaper Than Earlier Models*

The purchase price point of a fresh iPhone is nearly always a significant deciding factor as it pertains to if you should trade up, and regarding iPhone 11, this may be working for you. A new iPhone 11 clocks in at $699, which, for a brand-new model's release, seems pretty affordable. It's exceptionally sensible in comparison to the iPhone X's start price, which clocked in at $999, which makes it the priciest new iPhone model today. With this considered, taking the plunge into iPhone 11 and immediately doesn't appear so impossible.

If, after all, iPhone 11 provides sounds peachy by an up-front $699, continues to be unthinkable, the trade-in price for the iPhone 11 drops right down to only $399, or $17 monthly. There you own it, folks - only several most significant differences between your iPhone X and the iPhone 11. Only a reminder that post is evaluating the iPhone 11 with the iPhone X - the other iPhone 11 series models include additional features beyond those explained above and aren't one of them post, nevertheless, you can check them out here.

iPhone 11 vs iPhone XR assessment: What's the difference?

Apple announced the new iPhones at a meeting in Sept

2019, and like this past year, there are three new iPhones to choose from: the iPhone 11, iPhone 11 Pro, and iPhone 11 Pro Max. We have, in comparison, the three new models in another feature, but here we are considering the way the iPhone 11 comes even close to last year's iPhone XR.

Should you update from the iPhone XR, or if you have a mature iPhone, in the event you choose the iPhone XR or the iPhone 11 given, they may be for sale alongside one another?

- *Design*

iPhone 11: 150.9 x 75.7 x 8.3mm, 194g

iPhone XR: 150.9 x 75.7 x 8.3mm, 194g

The iPhone 11 and the iPhone XR both provide a similar design for the reason that they both come in several colours, offer an aluminum frame and a cup rear. There is a notch near the top of both their shows and they're identical in conditions of footprint and weight.

The iPhone XR is IP67 water-resistant, however, enabling it to be submerged up to one meter for thirty minutes, as the iPhone 11 is IP68 rated, offering submergence up to two-metres for thirty minutes. The iPhone 11 also offers a dual rear camera, with a camera casing that has frosted glass to differentiate it from all of those other glossy bodies and the Apple logo design techniques to the centre of the back, with the iPhone working removed entirely. The iPhone XR, in the meantime, has an individual back camera - making for the primary difference in design between both of these handsets - and it gets the Apple logo design higher up the back, as the iPhone branding rests towards underneath.

The colour options also differ between your iPhone 11 and iPhone XR, with the iPhone 11's colours more pastel in their approach and more beautiful because of this. The green and crimson options of the iPhone 11 are lovely, but we are big followers of the coral and blue options in the iPhone XR too.

- *Display*

iPhone 11: 6.1-inch, LCD, 1792 x 828 pixel resolution, no HDR, 625nits
iPhone XR: 6.1-inch, LCD, 1792 x 828 pixel resolution, no HDR, 625nits

Both iPhone 11 and the iPhone XR have a 6.1-in. Water Retina LCD screen, which has a 1792 x 828-pixel quality, producing a pixel denseness of 326ppi.

Nothing at all has changed in conditions of the display as it pertains to the cheaper iPhone models - the iPhone 11 and iPhone XR are identical. True Firmness technology continues to be on board, plus a wide colour gamut, and there continues to be Haptic Touch over 3D Touch. Neither device supplies the punch you will discover on the iPhone 11 Pro models or other OLED smartphones, and there is no HDR either, but you'd only spot the difference if you positioned them side-by-side basic other devices.

Normally, the iPhone 11 and iPhone XR deliver great shows with ample lighting and arguably more realistic colours in comparison to OLED panels.

- *Cameras*

iPhone 11: Tripple back camera (12MP wide position and ultra-wide position), 12MP TrueDepth front side camera

iPhone XR: Solitary back camera (12MP), 7MP

TrueDepth entrance camera

One of the primary differences between your iPhone 11 and the iPhone XR is their camera features, with the iPhone 11 the superior device.

The iPhone 11 has a dual-camera on the back, made up of a 12-megapixel ultra-wide-angle sensor with an aperture of f/2.4 and a wide-angle sensor with an aperture of f/1.8. There are optical image stabilization, a brighter True Shade flashes, and Family portrait Light with six results, as well as next-generation Smart HDR for photos. Additionally, there is Nighttime Mode and Auto Adjustments on the iPhone 11, but it is the Evening Mode that is the real stick out feature. The ultra-wide-angle sensor gives you to obtain additional in the shot than you'll get on the iPhone XR, but Night time Mode offers a substantial improvement in low light conditions in comparison to last year's model.

The iPhone XR meanwhile has an individually 12-megapixel rear camera with an f/1.8 aperture, optical image stabilization, and digital zoom up to 5x. Besides, it only offers three results for Portrait Light and first-gen Smart HDR for photos.

The iPhone XR also offers a 7-megapixel TrueDepth camera system with an aperture of f/2.2 on leading, enabling Face Identification, among a lot of other features. It includes 1080p video documenting at 30fps or 60fps.

The iPhone 11, in the meantime, has a 12-megapixel TrueDepth camera on leading, with an aperture of f/2.2, next-gen Smart HDR for photos, and 4K video saving at 24fps, 30fps and 60fps. Gleam slow-motion video option on the iPhone 11's front side camera, enabling what Apple phone calls *Slofies*. The truth is, this is a reasonably gimmicky feature - like Animoji and Memoji - nevertheless, you can have a blast with it.

- *Hardware*

iPhone 11: A13 chip, 64/256/512GB storage space, Dual SIM

iPhone XR: A12 chip, 64/256/512GB storage space, Dual SIM

Another primary difference between your iPhone 11 and the iPhone XR are hardware. As you'll expect, the iPhone 11 has a bump in hardware, moving from the A12 chip within the iPhone XR to the A13 chip. Both devices are easy in operation; however, the iPhone 11 offers a much better electric battery life than the iPhone XR, even although iPhone XR is, in fact, excellent still.

Both models come in 64GB, 256GB, and 512GB storage space options, though, and microSD for storage space expansion isn't on any model. Both devices support dual SIM with a nano-SIM and eSIM, and both devices are charged via Lightning. Besides, they both offer Apple Pay, plus they both offer 4G, however, not 5G features.

- *Software*

iPhone 11: iOS 13

iPhone XR: iOS 13 compatible

The iPhone 11 brings the release of iOS 13 with it; this means several new features including Dark Setting, a fresh Find My application that combines Find My Friends, and discover My iPhone collectively, a swiping keypad, an overhaul of Reminders and many other updates.

You can read about iOS 13 and what features it includes in greater detail inside our preview. The iPhone XR will also operate on iOS 13 when the program lands on 19 Sept so that it will offer you the same overall consumer experience as the iPhone 11.

The iPhone 11 has several features occasionally that are hardware-based - mainly in the camera department - and for that reason unavailable on the iPhone XR, but overall, the program experience between the unit is identical.

- *Price*

iPhone 11: From \$699/£729

iPhone XR: From \$599/£629

The iPhone 11 begins at \$699/£729, which is a little cheaper than the telephone XR started at when it launched this past year and every value in comparison with the iPhone 11 Pro models. The iPhone XR will be sold alongside the iPhone 11, starting at \$599/£629, which makes it a cheaper alternative.

Conclusion

The iPhone 11 has several upgrades on the iPhone XR, with the processor and camera features being the primary differences. The look remains mainly the same between your two devices, though, and the screen and software experience is just about identical too.

Improving from the iPhone XR to the iPhone 11, therefore, only offers a lift in camera - that will be enough for a few - and an increase in rate, but in addition to that, you'll get a fairly similar experience this time. Upgrading from a mature iPhone to either the iPhone XR or iPhone 11 will offer you a lot of differences, though you will have to decide if you would like to spend the excess £100 for the camera and processor boosts in the iPhone 11.

The iPhone 11 is an excellent device; however, the iPhone XR is too, so it's possible you'll be happy with either. When you can spend the money for extra £100, the iPhone 11's Evening Mode and supplementary ultra-wide-angle zoom lens are worthwhile, as well as the prolonged battery pack life, but you won't be disappointed with the iPhone XR as it's still a great performer and great value now.

CHAPTER 26

How to Watch Pandora Channels Offline

Are you a **Pandora** lover?

I will help you make your playlists to be accessible offline. Doing work to save lots of some music on your mobile phone doesn't take much space for storage to your device, and stored tunes are an exquisite component to have access whenever you're short of data bundle/tariff connection, but need to hear music to resolve your boredom problem. The feature works on **Google android** and **iOS devices**.

If you've not made your playlists available offline, doing this is quite exceptionally easy and can be carried out in only a few moments.

One important caveat: You need to be considered a paid customer to Pandora through Pandora Plus ($5/month) or even to Pandora Premium ($10/month.) you can view the programs on Pandora's website.

Without further ado, follow the instructions below;

- I recommend linking your phone to a wireless connection. You can download songs more than a mobile data connection instead of cellular, but it's heading to have a reasonable level of data utilization to get the whole lot downloaded. When you have the option of connecting to a WiFi network, please do this because it can save you more time with regards to the truth that Wi-Fi is faster than mobile data generally in most conditions.

- Start the ***Pandora app***.

- Making channels available offline requires you to have channels to be produced offline undoubtedly. If you haven't made any channels on Pandora, have a short while to make a few. You'll also have to pay attention to them for at least a few tunes so that Pandora considers them your favourites.

- Tap the three lines located at the very top left facet of the app so that you can gain access to Pandora's menu. At the lowest area of the screen, you'll see an "offline setting" slider. Slide that pub to initiate offline settings for your tool. When you do, Pandora will synchronize your top 4 channels on your smartphone and lead them to be accessible offline.

At first attempt, I'd advise that you let your mobile phone stay connected to the Wi-Fi network for approximately 30 minutes to make everything synchronize. How fast things happen depends on the speed of your web connection.

When the whole tune is synchronized, on every occasion you will need to hear songs offline, you need to visit that menu, and you will toggle the offline button ON. The application will remain in an offline setting until you situate it back to the conventional configuration.

Why Should Pandora Station be Used in Offline Mode?

You can focus on Pandora each day you are at home.

You could have a radio train station for when you're running, another for enough time you are strolling out with your dogs, plus some other for if you are working from home doing some jogging. You can similarly have a route you dedicate for just about any social gathering you host.

I take benefit of offline mode because I like to visit a lot of different countries, which is an incredible enjoyment, aside from the cellular phone expenses. Whenever I am on a journey, I try to use only a small amount of mobile data as you possibly would want to stay away from the high cost of use that comes by the end of the month, but slicing out specific applications like *Pandora*.

Why should I exclude using Pandora, especially in conventional mode or online mode?

That is done because streaming music occupies the right amount of data bundle, due to this, it's off-limit for individuals with limited data plans (luckily, unlimited when at home). Additionally, you lose out on hearing when you're in places like aircraft and trains where your computer data connection is either sluggish or non-existent.

Chapter 27

How to Fix Common iPhone 11 Problems

iPhone 11 Touch Screen Issues

The bright, beautiful *"edge-to-edge"* OLED screen on the iPhone is one of its major new features; however, the touch screen may sometimes go wrong. Both most common situations are:

✓ *Non-responsive SCREEN AND "GHOST TOUCHES."*

Some users state that the screen on the iPhone 11 sometimes halts working. In those instances, the screen doesn't react to details or touches. In other situations, the contrary occurs: "ghost details" appear to activate things on the screen even when they don't touch it.

If you are experiencing either of these issues, the reason is the same: a hardware problem with the touch screen chips and detectors in the iPhone 11; because these problems are the effect of a hardware issue, you can't fix them yourself. Fortunately, Apple knows the problem and offers to repair it. Find out about how to proceed on Apple's web page about the issue.

✓ *Frozen Screen in Winter*

A different type of iPhone 11 screen problem that many people run into would be that the screen freezes up and becomes unresponsive for a couple of seconds when going from a warm spot to a chilly one (such as moving out into a wintery day). The good thing is that this is not a hardware problem, so it is much simpler to fix. Try out these quick DIY fix:

- *Update the iOS*: This issue was set with the iOS 11.1.2 update, so make sure you're operating that version of the operating system or higher.

- *Follow Apple's Cold-Weather Recommendations*: Apple has tips and recommendations for the temperatures to use the iPhone in, it suggests not using it in temperature ranges less than 32 degrees F (0 degrees C). Having your iPhone within your clothes and near to your body, warmth is an excellent, simple fix.

iPhone 11 Loudspeaker Problems

The iPhone is a great multimedia device; however, many users report reduced enjoyment of media on the iPhone 11 credited to speaker problems. Listed below are two of the very most common.

a) *Speakers Audio Muffled*

Speakers whose audio is quiet than they ought to, or whose audio sounds muffled, can frequently be fixed by doing the next:

- *Restart iPhone*: Restarting your iPhone can solve all types of problems, including sound issues.

- *Clean the Speakers*. You might have dirt or other gunk developed on the loudspeakers that are leading to the quietness. Understand how to completely clean iPhone speakers.

- *Check the Case*: If you are using a case with your iPhone, make sure there is nothing stuck between your case and the loudspeaker, like pocket lint, that may be causing the problem.

b) *Loudspeaker crackles at high volume*

Around the other end of the range, some iPhone 11 users have reported that their speakers make a distressing crackling sound when their volume is too high. If this is going on for you, try the next steps:

- *Restart iPhone*: It might not assist in this case, but it's fast and straightforward, so that it never hurts to get one of this restart. You can also get one of these hard reset if you want.

- *Update the OS*: Because the latest version of the iOS also includes the latest bug fixes, make sure you're operating it.

- *Talk with Apple*: Crackling loudspeakers are likely to be always a hardware problem that you can't solve. Get active support from Apple instead.

Some individuals have encountered problems using Wi-Fi on the iPhone 11. It probably isn't a concern with the iPhone 11 itself. Much more likely, this has regarding software configurations or your Wi-Fi network. Find out about the complexities and fixes in How exactly to Fix an iPhone That Can't Hook up to Wi-Fi in other recommended books at the end of this book.

iPhone 11 Charging Problems

The iPhone 11 is the first iPhone to add support for wireless charging. That's cool, but it isn't cool if the telephone won't charge properly. If you are facing that problem, try these steps to repair it:

- *Get one of these New Charging Cable*: Maybe the charging issue has been your wire, not your phone. Try another cable you know for sure works. Make sure to either uses the official Apple cable or one that's qualified by Apple.

- *Remove Credit cards From Case*: If you are wanting to charge cellular and have an instance that also stores things such as credit cards, take away the credit cards. The mobile payment top features of the credit cards can hinder the mobile charging.

- ***Remove Case for Wifi Charging***: Removing the whole case may be considered a good idea if you are charging wirelessly. Not absolutely all cases are appropriate for cellular charging, so that they may be avoiding normal function.

- ***Restart iPhone***: You never know very well what types of problems a restart can solve. This may be one of them.

iPhone 11 Electric battery Life Problems

There is nothing worse than not having the ability to use your mobile phone because it's working out of electric battery too early, but that's the thing some users complain about. And with most of its fresh, power-hungry features - the OLED screen, for example - it isn't a shock that there could be some iPhone 11 electric battery problems.

Fortunately, battery issues on the iPhone are simple enough to solve using the settings included in iOS. Below are a few tips:

- *Learn to Preserve Battery*: There are over 30+ tips about how to raise your iPhone's electric battery life. Use a few of these as well as your iPhone would run much longer between charges.

- *Update the OS*: Furthermore, to fix a bug, new variations of iOS often deliver improvements that make the battery better. Install the latest revise, and you'll see your electric battery last longer.

- *Get a protracted Life Electric battery*: Maybe the simplest way to get your electric battery to go longer is to obtain additional battery. There are sorts of prolonged life batteries on the marketplace, from exterior dongles to others.

iPhone 11 Face ID Problems

Most likely, the single coolest feature of the iPhone 11 is the facial ID, the facial recognition system. This feature is utilized for security and convenience: it unlocks the telephone, can be used to enter passwords, and even authorizes Apple Pay transactions. But issues with Face ID and either front or back camera can cause your iPhone 11 never to identify you. If you are (ahem) facing this issue, try these pointers:

- *Adjust iPhone Position*: If Face ID sometimes identifies you, but other times doesn't, consider changing the position you're holding the telephone. As the Face ID sensors are relatively sophisticated, they need to be capable of getting a good view of that person to work.

- *Clean "The Notch."*: THE FACIAL ID detectors are situated in "the notch," the deep cut-out near the top of the screen. If those receptors get protected with dirt or even enough oil from your skin layer, their standard procedure could be reduced. Try wiping "the notch" clean.

- *Update the OS*: Apple regularly enhances the speed and precision of Face ID, as well as fixes insects, in new variations of the iOS. If you are having Face ID problems on iPhone 11, make sure you're using the latest operating system.

- _Reset Face ID_: The problem is probably not with Face ID itself, but instead with the initial scans of that person created when you set up Face ID to start. If the other activities haven't helped, be rid of your old face scans and make new ones. Enter a shiny, well-lit place and then go to Configurations -> Face ID & Passcode -> enter your passcode -> Reset Face ID. Then create Face ID from scratch.

- _Contact Apple_: If none of the things has helped, there may be a problem with the hardware in your iPhone 11 (maybe it's a problem with the video cameras, the Face ID sensors, or another thing). If so, you should contact Apple to obtain an analysis of the problem and a fix.

- _You might have seen tales on the internet claiming that Face ID has been hacked_: They are virtually all bogus. Face ID can be an extremely advanced system that depends on thousands of data factors to identify a face. Yes, similar twins might be able to beat Face ID (it seems sensible; they have simply the same face!). Other families that look nearly the same as one another can also be able to technique it. But also, for the most part, the probability of Face ID being tricked or hacked is very, surprisingly low.

iPhone 11 Screen Issues

The iPhone 11 was the first iPhone to use the brighter, better OLED screen technology. The screen appears excellent, but it's susceptible to some issues that other iPhones using different systems aren't. Perhaps most obviously among these is "burn off in."; this happens when the same image is shown on a screen for an extended period, resulting in faint "spirits" of these images showing up on the screen regularly, regardless of what else has been screened. Fortunately, OLED burn-in is simple to avoid. Just follow these pointers:

- *Lower Screen Lighting*: The lower the lighting of

your screen, the less likely a graphic burn off involved with it. You have two options here. First, you can by hand reduce your screen brightness by starting Control Centre and moving the lighting slider down. On the other hand, let your screen brightness change to ambient light by heading to *Configurations -> General -> Convenience -> Screen brightness -> Auto-Brightness*.

- *Set Screen to Auto-Lock*: Burn off happens when a graphic is on the screen for an extended period. So, if your screen hair and shuts off regularly, the image can't burn off. Set your screen to lock by heading to Configurations automatically -> Screen & Lighting -> Auto-Lock and choose five minutes or less.

Another screen problem that impacts some iPhone 11 models is a green line that appears at the right edge of the screen. That is another hardware problem that users can't fix themselves. If you see this, your very best wager is to get hold of Apple to get active support.

LET US HEAR FROM YOU!

We love testimonies. We love to hear what your opinions are from the information you have read in this author's book. Please share your experience and lesson learnt from this book with us, as we look forward always to serve you better.

Also, *please consider giving this book a **good review** on the product page where you purchased, and check out other books by the same author and other book recommendations by our publishing house.*

We also invite you to check out our website at http://www.engolee.com/bookdeals and consider joining our newsletter growing list of hundreds of thousands of book lovers, which we send **Free and Discounted books** too weekly, with great tips, testimonies and resourceful content from the various authors that connect with us.

Feel free to drop us your suggestions, opinions, testimonies etc. at info@engolee.com We would be eager to listen and support you, and also work on any advice given to us.

OTHER BOOKS BY PUBLISHING HOUSE

1. iPhone Guide: The Simplified Manual for Kids and Adult

2. iPhone: The User Manual like No Other

3. iPhone 6s: A Guide To iPhone 6S for All Ages: The User Manual like No Other

4. iPhone 6s Plus: The Ultimate Guide to Revolutionizing Your iPhone Mobile: The User Manual like No Other

5. Apple Watch Series: The Ultimate Guide For All Apple Watch Band Series Users: The User manual Like No Other

6. iPad Pro: The Beginners, Kids and Expert Guide to iPad Pro 12.9 and Other Versions: The User Manual like No Other

7. iPhone: Making the Most Use of Your iPhone Features with Simplicity

8. iPhone Unusual: The Manual for Smart Users

9. iPhone Guide: Maximizing the Future of Cell Phone Technology

10. iPhone Plus: The Instant Solution to Under-Using of iPhone

11. iPad: The User Manual like No Other

12. iPad Guide: The Simplified Manual for Kids and Adult

13. Apple Watch Series 5: The Simplified User Manual for iWatch Series 5 Owners: The Simplified Manual for Kids and Adult

14. iPad: Making the Most Use of Your iPad Features with Simplicity

15. iPad Unusual: The Manual for Smart Users

16. iPad Guide: Maximizing the Future of Tablets Devices

17. iPad: The Instant Solution to Under-Using of iPad

Tablets Devices

18. <u>iPad Guide:</u> The Informative Manual For all iPad Mini, iPad Air, and iPad Pro Users: The Simplified Manual for Kids and Adult

19. <u>Allergy & Asthma Relief:</u> #1 Straight to Point Solution for Managing Asthma Attack Symptoms, Signs and Causes in Children and Adult

20. <u>Allergy No More:</u> The Concise Solution for Managing Symptoms, Signs and Causes of Drugs, Food, Insect, Latex, Mold, Pet, Pollen, Skin, and Dirt Allergies for Kids and Adults

21. <u>Anxiety & Phobia Crushed:</u> The Summarized Approach to Combat Anxiety and Regain your Life

22. <u>Asthma Relief:</u> The Summarized Fail-proof Asthma Attack Care Therapy

23. <u>Baby Sign Language Simplified:</u> A Natural Way to Start Communicating with Your Child

Disposable Baby Diapers with Effective Potty Training Strategies

32. Instant Potty Training: Child-friendly Key Strategies to Help You Toilet Train Your Preschooler Quickly and Successfully

33. Potty Chairs: Effective Guide for Choosing a Perfect Potty Chair

34. Toddler Potty: Consumer Guide for Choosing The Best Potty Chair for Boys & Girls

35. Happy Kids Potty Training: Simple, Smart, and Effective Solutions to Your Child's Potty Struggles [3 Days Strategy]

36. Potty Chair: The Art of Choosing The Best Toddler/Kids Portable Potty

37. Potty Seat For Toddlers: The Art of Choosing The Best Toddler Seats

38. Potty Training Seats: How to Know & Choose the Best Potty Seat Suitable for Your Child

39. <u>Potty Training Simplified:</u> Key Strategies for Potty Learning that Foster Healthy Brain Development for Babies, Toddlers & Kids

40. <u>Pet Dog Natural Training:</u> Revolutionize Your Puppy & Dog Training in 14 Days with these easy-peasy Tips

41. <u>Dog Training Smackdown:</u> The A - Z of Puppy & Dog Training

42. <u>Cracking the Dog Training Code:</u> Make Your Dog Training a Reality

43. <u>DOG TRAINING INNOVATION:</u> The Sure-Fire Approach to Raising the Best Pet

INDEX

CPSIA information can be obtained
at www.ICGtesting.com
Printed in the USA
LVHW021459160320
650185LV00001B/104

9 781710 240092